REVIEV

HEAD STRONG:

Through Life, Love and Brain Surgery

I work with many authors to help them get their story out to the world. I am incredibly proud and honored to have worked with Heather and her wonderful parents as this story evolved into the book you are holding in your hands now. Of all the books I have been involved with, this book is one of the most inspiring I have ever read. Heather is courageous, determined and has a true heart to use the setbacks and challenges in her life as a way to inspire people and help them transform their own lives. Headstrong will have a global impact on many people and I look forward to working with Heather for many years to come.

—Andrew Jobling, Bestselling Author and *International motivational speaker*

***

Heather's life journey is an incredible testimony of God's desire to walk with each of us in the midst of extreme pain, difficult circumstances and life-altering tragedies. Her story is a beautiful illustration of how a raw faith in God can overcome the brutal reality of this broken world.

As a girl dad, I was especially drawn to Heather's invitation to her parents to honestly respond in each chapter. Watching their daughter go through these horrendous trials, they could have easily grown bitter and thrown in the faith towel, but instead they fought to trust God with an incredible church community surrounding their entire family.

Head Strong is truly an inspiring story to the kind of faith I want for my family.

—Kent Chevalier, *Pittsburgh Steelers Chaplain*

***

If you want to know what it's like to experience God's love amid tragedy, this book is a definitive account. While Heather's physical body struggled, this book highlights the determination and grit it took to begin a new normal successfully. I was at the hospital; I heard the doctors' difficult conversations. However, I also witnessed the God changing moments and saw the human spirit thrive. I recommend this book because there isn't another on the market that captures the way to become Head Strong.

—Scott Stevens, Pastor, *North Way Christian Community*

***

You don't know how strong you are until "strong" is your only option.

Facing mortality at the threshold of adulthood thrust Heather and her family into years of life-or-death decisions.

For Heather's parents it was having to imagine the unimaginable, day after day, night after night. Their daughter could die at any moment. They did not know who to turn to for help or who to trust. Still, Lynn and Randy defied the paralyzing prognosis given to their daughter. They took action and made one hard decision after another to help their daughter stay alive.

For Heather it was more than her determination to stay alive. **Head Strong** is about Heather's decision to create dreams bigger and beyond what she could have imagined before her world changed with her first brain bleed.

Heather's story will give you hope and inspiration on how to live the life you have today to your fullest potential and believe in what looks to others as impossible.

—**Joyce Strong,** RN, *BSN Holistic RN Coach*

***

We are fortunate that such a remarkable person has shared her insight and experience of her imminently life threatening and life altering experience. Challenges in life are not easy and Head Strong will provide you with a roadmap. A must read.

—**Robert M. Friedlander,** MD, MA

Chairman Department of Neurological Surgery

Walter Dandy Endowed Professor of Neurosurgery and Neurobiology

University of Pittsburgh School of Medicine

University of Pittsburgh Medical Center

HEAD STRONG:

Through Life, Love, and Brain Surgery

HEATHER L. RENDULIC

Published by KHARIS PUBLISHING, imprint of KHARIS MEDIA LLC.

Copyright © 2020 Heather L. Rendulic

ISBN-13: 978-1-946277-86-2
ISBN-10: 1-946277-86-X

Library of Congress Control Number: 2020950528

All KHARIS PUBLISHING products are available at special quantity discounts for bulk purchase for sales promotions, premiums, fund-raising, and educational needs. For details, contact:

Kharis Media LLC
Tel: 1-479-599-8657
support@kharispublishing.com
www.kharispublishing.com

CONTENTS

Foreword

As long as I can remember I wanted to be a doctor. I have always been fascinated with how the body works. To understand how our amazing body works, it takes a lot of early studying with a progressive level of specialization. It all starts as early as elementary school and into high school, learning basic biology, chemistry and physics.

In many colleges, a significant portion of entering freshman declare a premed interest, with only a fraction completing the requirements, and only a fraction of them gaining acceptance into medical school.

Medical school consists of four grueling years in which the student learns both the basics of how the body functions, (health) and also how the body malfunctions (disease). During these four years, medical students decide what their specialty will be. As you can imagine, sometimes the decision is simple, sometimes more difficult. What is clear is that it takes a significant amount of work and dedication to reach this stage. Furthermore, to reach these milestones, physicians have had to be at the top of their classes to achieve admission into these extremely competitive and coveted positions.

For me, my path after medical school took me into neurosurgery. I had to choose one of the longest and most competitive specialties. Why did I want to spend my 20s and early 30s studying and working as a resident for sometimes 120 hours per week? Missing out on the best years of my life, while my high school and college friends were already in the "real world," starting families, having the opportunity to participate in a social life, and advancing their careers? The reason I made all these sacrifices (which I didn't consider a sacrifice) was to have the honor to be able to take care of people like Heather. What an honor and a burden to have the trust of a peer human being, to be entrusted with physically entering into the middle of their brain to fix a problem.

I first met Heather and her wonderful family after she had an initial bleed into her brainstem. As you may surmise, the stem of the brain is an extremely important structure. It is the connection between the brain and the rest of the body and the connection between the rest of the body and the brain. It has additional, incredibly important functions, among them being awake, breathing, and heart rate. Not only is the brain stem really important, but it also is incredibly densely packed. Each millimeter has a function. There is no millimeter to spare. Therefore, lesions in the brainstem can cause devastating damage. By extension, operating on the brainstem is extremely risky.

Heather "had" a cavernous malformation in her brainstem. Some lesions in the brainstem are safer to remove, but others are more risky. When Heather presented, her lesion was on the "more risky" side. The challenge with such lesions is to determine whether there is a safe surgical corridor to reach the lesion and remove it. Traditional MRI studies provide information on the precise location of the lesion. It does not provide information on how the lesion has affected the normal brain pathways. The question is whether the lesion severed the pathways, or just displaced them. If they are displaced, in which direction are they being displaced, medial lateral anterior or posterior? This is key information because it alters the trajectory, I could take to remove the cavernoma and not damage the function of her brain. Most precisely, with Heather, I was most concerned with the movement of the left side of her body.

At the University of Pittsburgh and UPMC, we have developed an advanced imaging technique that provides me with the information I need to determine with precision (not guess) where these important fibers are located. We call this technique HDFT, high definition fiber tracking. The information I attained from Heather's HDFT study resulted in my decision that, at that point, the operation was too risky. If brain fibers are cut, they do not return. If fibers are displaced by a new bleed, they may or may not recover. It all depends on the severity of the bleed.

After agonizing and careful consideration, we decided not to operate on the cavernoma but rather treat it with Gamma Knife, which is non-invasive focused radiation. It has been shown to reduce the likelihood of cavernomas to bleed. However, there is controversy as to its effi-cacy; the protection is not complete, and there is a lag time from radi-ation to a reduction in hemorrhage risk. Much of the data providing support for the use of Gamma Knife for cavernomas have been gen-erated at the University of Pittsburgh by my colleague, Dr. L. Dade Lunsford. He first introduced Gamma Knife in North America in 1987 and is a clear visionary in the field.

Approximately one month after Gamma Knife, Heather had two more significant bleeds within a few days apart. At this point, she had sig-nificant weakness and numbness on the left side of her body. The new bleed caused significant damage. It was unclear if the damage was per-manent, or if Heather had a chance to recover. The overwhelming likelihood is that she likely sustained grave, permanent damage to her brain.

Repeat HDFT imaging revealed a small corridor for me to be able to remove the offending lesion. The goal of surgery was to remove the cavernoma. Additional bleeding would likely be devastating. The sur-gery was very risky as well. She could be permanently paralyzed, una-ble to eat, breathe without support, and have permanent double vision, among other very serious consequences. After careful consideration, this was the right time to go into surgery. The support for her and trust of me from her amazing family was remarkable through these very dif-ficult times. However, what was most remarkable was how Heather dealt with this dire situation. Many patients dealing with such a devas-tating threat to their livelihood become defeated. No matter what the odds were against her recovery, Heather always had a beautiful smile and a positive attitude. There was no question in her mind that she was going to win this war against this aggressive cavernoma.

As I tell my patients, 50% of the recovery process is controlled by their positive attitude, by a strong desire to do as well as possible. I did not have to tell this to Heather. She was all in, and was going to do what it took to get through this challenge. She sure did.

The surgery was an extreme success. A few days after surgery, she went to the Neurorehabilitation Center at Mercy UPMC. After months of hard work, and her positive attitude, Heather walked back into my office. I was so happy for her and her family to see how much progress she had made.

Seeing what a difference I can make in someone's life is so much more than enough payoff for all the years and long hours of training. What a privilege it is to be able to be entrusted by my patients to take care of the organ that makes them who they are. Every time I see a brain, I am in awe of what I am about to do. Having the privilege to be entrusted by Heather and every single one of my patients provides me the determination to continue to improve every day.

Heather's amazing positive attitude, even against immeasurable odds, is a true inspiration to me. Her story, in her own words, will provide strength to many others facing adversity. What a thrill to see Heather sharing her soul, her private life, through this inspirational book.

Robert M. Friedlander, MD, MA

Chairman, Department of Neurological Surgery

Walter Dandy Endowed Professor of Neurosurgery and Neurobiology

University of Pittsburgh School of Medicine

University of Pittsburgh Medical Center

Co-Director UPMC Neurological Institute

Address:

UPMC Presbyterian Hospital

Fourth Floor

Suite B449

Pittsburgh, PA 15213

Phone: 412-647-6358

Introduction

What is your worst nightmare? Well, mine happened to me about seven years ago. I was a healthy, 22-year-old college student with the world at her feet. Then I had five strokes over 11 months. You read that correctly: Five strokes, and 22 years old. I found myself fighting for my life and trying to comprehend why this happened to me. I was completely paralyzed on my left side, and the picture of my life I have had since I was a kid had suddenly crashed and burned. I was left with two options: Give up or fight.

Through the following pages you will find out what choice I made and gain insights into my thought process along the way. I start by laying out the groundwork to my life; growing up, I had experiences and impactful things that influenced who I am as a person. I truly believe we all have things in life that shape us as people. Whether it be a good thing or bad thing, we are molded by experiences and people in our lives.

After I laid out my groundwork, I experienced a life- changing diagnosis that changed my future, something that rocked me and my family to the core, and forever changed our lives. I continued to suffer, from bad news to more bad news, which took me to my breaking point.

I wrote this book to help inspire people across the world. I have full faith that God sent me through my tragic journey and subsequent revival to share it with the world. It is too good of a story not to share!

This book is intended for all audiences and people. As people, we all experience difficulties; no one difficulty is less severe than the other. They all impact us, and we must learn how to prevail, despite the difficulty! I hope you enjoy my journey…

The Dawn

October 25, 1989 is where it all began. I was brought into this world and, like every baby, had no clue what to expect. But I guess we all don't really care either. I had two loving parents, a roof over my head, and food in my belly. I did have something rather unusual about me, but we will get to that later. I had a normal childhood, but oh, how I hate that word "normal." Instead, I'll say I had a "what is to be expected" childhood. My parents provided my older sister and me with everything we could need, and more. I was blessed.

When I was about two years old, recently potty trained (trust me this comes into play later), my sister started taking horseback riding lessons. As I continued being a potty-trained toddler, it was really getting in my way of playing. I found an intense game of Leggos™ got rudely interrupted by having to stop and go to the bathroom. So logically, I decided that it was too much work to go to the toilet to, you know, so I regressed to wearing diapers again. As any younger sibling does, I was jealous of my sister riding horses and demanded I get the chance to do the same. My mother, being the intelligent woman she is, used this desire in me to make a business deal. Mom pleaded, "Heather, if you go potty on the toilet like a big girl, then I'll let you ride a pony!"

Well played, Mom!

So, I plopped myself down on that potty and waited for the magic to happen. Sure, enough it did, and thus transpired one of the most embarrassing home videos of me to date. I ran downstairs yelling "I went pee pee on the potty!!!!! I get to ride Pony now!!" Oh, if only other things we want in life were that simple to get. What a world that would

1

be to live in. But to me this was a big deal; it marked the start of my passion for horseback riding, all while using the proper methods of going to the bathroom.

Riding became a whole family activity. I always thought horseback riding was only for the wealthy. This is not always the case, and I have to say that in the equestrian world of things, we were "poor." For those of you who don't know what I am talking about, it's this: We bought "budget" horses, mucked our own stalls, and wore old clothing to the barn. Oh, the horror! To further my defense, there were other people at the barn who bought horses for over $100,000 and had hired help who mucked their stalls and got their horses ready for them, so when they showed up in their equestrian designer clothes, they could just hop on and ride their Mercedes with fur and four legs. Not everyone at our stables was like this, but they did stick out like a shiny penny. Especially to me.

As my riding career developed, I envied these people who seemed to have it all together. They got to own the fancy horses, travel to all the big horse shows, and I was just doing the best with what I had. I had a talent for the sport. At times, it felt as though no matter how good a rider I was, I could not succeed without my parents spending more money. This led to resentment and feeling inadequate, compared to my friends in the sport who had the fancier horses and got to travel to all the big equestrian events. Did their parents love them more than mine did? Why is my dad so cheap? Can't he see this is my passion?

Enter a very valuable lesson: If you want something, you have to work very hard for it. This seems like common sense, but I found myself determined to go to college and get a degree that would provide me with the opportunity to make money and have all those nice things and fancy horses. Nothing in life is given to us. Maybe my dad was just teaching me a lesson that he wasn't just going to give me everything and anything I wanted. He knew life didn't work like that.

What I learned, when I was in the midst of the unequal money being spent between me and my friends in the barn, was that all I could see was how unfair it was and feel jealous. Little did I know it would help push me to work harder in school, get a college degree, and take matters into my own hands. Would I have pursued a college degree without this driving force? I would never know, but it certainly didn't hurt!

My parents loved me more than anything and gave me more than I ever deserved, but it was me comparing myself to others that was the problem. We need to learn to just be content with what we have and stop comparing ourselves to other people. Find the joy in today; find the joy in what you have right now. You have more right now than some people in this world will ever have. I'll take a shot in the dark here, but I bet, if you made a list of all the things you *do* have right now, it will be much longer than all the things you want to have. Sure, it's still good to have wants in your life; heck that is what motivates us to try hard every day. But when we get that feeling of focusing on all the things we *don't* have, that can be just plain depressing!

Now back to my backstory. Another impactful experience from my childhood had to be the amount of travel on which I got to embark. No, we didn't vacation in Europe, or safari in Africa (but this is on my bucket list), but I got to see different parts of the country and the world. Of course, at the time this did not seem significant, but if you are paying attention to the theme of this chapter, you will see there is a reason for my madness. This traveling enabled me to see there was a whole world outside my neighborhood. Although it was a very nice neighborhood, it opened my eyes to the endless possibilities within the world and it made me realize that traveling is quite fun! These experiences also motivated me to get a degree and make a nice life for myself.

Horseback riding was a staple in my growing up years. To be quite honest, it got me through some very difficult times. My mom graced me with her depression gene. (*Thanks Mom!*) It struck me when I was in fifth grade, roughly 11 years old. Most 11-year-olds are working on their monkey bar skills, and here I was, working on my emotions with a psychologist. Depression hit me out of nowhere and I remember just suddenly feeling like I was not motivated anymore; I had no joy. It was if a dark cloud just randomly plopped over my head and I couldn't seem to shake it.

Only a few weeks after starting my depression journey, I went to Mexico on a foreign exchange program through my elementary school. Probably not the best timing, right? But I was in Mexico, and

3

to my surprise, I was assigned to a family who did not speak any English. The daughter knew some English, but the rest of the family did not speak one word. This, coupled with being in a foreign country that is much different than America, did not turn out well. The family was nice, but I was extremely homesick and feeling so afraid. I only lasted a few days before I could not bear to be away from home any longer and my mom came to my rescue, as she always does. She flew down to Mexico and brought me back home.

It was tough, especially when you are so young and did not understand chemical imbalances in your brain. Nor was it something I could openly talk about with friends; they would treat me like I had the plague. Unfortunate, but true. Well, my battle with depression taught me a lot of important life lessons at a very young age. First, it taught me just how ruthless depression is when picking its victims. I was 11 years old, had parents who loved me, a roof over my head, and everything I could ever need, yet I felt so immensely sad and hopeless. Depression also taught me how to better understand my emotional well-being, express my emotions, and feel comfortable talking about them with others. Last, depression taught me that no matter how sad and hopeless I feel, these feelings will pass. At times, these feelings are suffocating, and it feels like they are never-ending, but I can assure you these bouts of extreme emotion *are* temporary and *will* pass eventually. All you must do is breathe. Seems pretty simple, right?

I entered middle school on antidepressants, splattered with acne, and already wearing a B-cup bra. I was a perfect candidate to be bullied. In the peak of my "awkward stage," it seemed appropriate to assume I would be bullied. No one, and I mean *no one* should be bullied. More of my thoughts on this later, but first to my experience. I was not part of the cool crowd. Actually, I was not part of any particular crowd at all. I was just a middle school student. I mostly kept to myself and had trouble making friends. I never have been good at those conversations you have with people you barely know. I always get nervous and embarrass myself. Goals to work on, I guess.

Eventually, I did find friends who were what my mother would call, "promiscuous." Does every mom use that word? It was that weird phase of puberty and all the hormones. I did not partake in all the activities of these friends, but definitely associated with them. This was when I learned people will judge you by those with whom you associate. My parents did not approve of these friends and I distanced myself from them. I cannot be positive, but I am pretty sure this was where my bullying started.

The "friends" were disgruntled with me distancing myself and started some ridiculous untrue rumors. Anyone who has had a rumor spread about them can relate to how hurtful they are. Next came the bullying, people calling me horrible and nasty names, names so horrible they should have had their mouths washed out with a bar of soap. I won't go into detail about some of the things that were said, considering my sweet grandmother is probably reading this book.

Love you, Gamma.

Because of all the bullying, I hated going to school. I felt attacked, humiliated, disliked by all, and quite frankly unsafe. Thus, I started getting really good at faking the whole, "Mom, my tummy hurts," act and staying home from school a lot. Unfortunately, things would need to get worse before they got better.

My depression skyrocketed. Feeling like such an outcast in school can do crazy things to a person. As depression does best, I started to believe what these people were saying and to blame it on myself. I was a horrible, ugly person and people were mean to me because I deserved it. Crazy, right? Well, it made sense to me at the time and I started to self-mutilate as a form of punishment. Yes, that means cutting myself. I was in such a dark place that I truly thought hurting my own body would somehow make things better. News flash, it did not make me feel any better, only worse.

I continued seeing my therapist. After many tough sessions, we made progress and I stopped the cutting. I tried to convince my parents I needed to be home-schooled. Then I wouldn't have to face these mean people anymore and I would be happy. "I know you don't want to go to school honey, but it is the best place for you, and you'll thank us one day," Mom said while she hugged me.

What mean parents, right? Well, I went back and pushed through the remaining time in middle school and moved on to high school. Surprisingly enough, high school was much better and the bullying stopped. Must've gotten bored of me or something. My parents taught me another very valuable lesson: You cannot run away from your problems. They could've home-schooled me, but instead, they made me confront my problems head on and conquer my fears. They knew that I would figure out how to handle school with bullies.

People can be so cruel in this world. Unfortunately, while it is inevitable that people will be mean to you at some point, it is in your hands how you react to those bullies. Me taking people's words to affect how I valued myself was not the right way to react.

You are so valuable, there is only one you in this whole world! Coming from experience, I can promise you that things will get better, and one day you will realize those peoples' words meant nothing and were all lies.

In high school, I still only had a couple close friends, most of whom did not go to my school, but I met through horseback riding. I kept to myself and focused on riding and had an occasional boyfriend to liven things up a little. My parents loved the boyfriend phase.

Mom here

Just a few thoughts.

Thank-you Heather for thinking my plan about the pony and potty training was intelligent. When you plopped yourself down right away I thought, "Oh crap, (excuse the pun) now I have to put my two-year-old on the back of a pony! What was I thinking?" As it did turn out, riding helped shape you into the strong person you are today. Your ability to coexist with a 1200-pound animal gave you the confidence you would need. In addition, that hard work of mucking stalls taught you that there is satisfaction in a job well done. Moreover, we love that horsey smell.

The depression gene goes way back in our family history. It is a hard and, at times, ugly thing. I have been there and understand the blackness and despair you felt. Once you work your way through, as you said, there are lessons to be learned and a realization of the strength you never knew you had. Little did I know that was not the last time genes would play a significant part in your life.

Last, the bullying was a very hard thing for a Mom to see her child go through. It also happened before the true effects of bullying were recognized. I spoke with parents, school officials, and teachers, but it was a time when the thought was "kids will be kids." As I later became aware, watching that pain and anguish you were going through, while it was difficult for me, the future would show me that Heather had more inner strength than I ever realized.

Parenting is a challenge, but also a blessing. We are all doing the very best we can. We will never shield our children from all adversity, nor should we. This is a marathon and not a sprint so breathe deep and stay strong.

Dad here

Thoughts and perspective.

When you were born, the doctor announced, "It's a girl," and on my birthday. I could not have been more excited, thinking that a girl could not be as challenging as I was as a boy growing up. You certainly blew up that assumption pretty quickly.

Though I totally understand your equestrian dilemma, I don't believe the use of "Cheap and Horses" is anything other than an oxymoron. However, it was the greatest family experience that I will always cherish, especially the Thanksgiving trip (only weeks before your medical problems arose) in ARUBA, and we galloped horses with your Mom and I on the beach.

As a Dad, all we can do is love our children, provide for them the best we can, set limits, and always strive to be a good example. Heather you have consistently shown you have learned from life experiences, good and bad, always fighting through with God's help. For this, I could not be more proud of you.

The Love

So my first "love," we shall call Jeff. Don't worry, I am not going to go through every relationship I've had in my life, just the ones I feel are significant in my story. Sorry to the guys who didn't make the cut... ouch. Did you notice in the first sentence of this paragraph how the word love is in quotation marks? I did that because, looking back on this relationship, it was clearly not love at all. But we are all young once, so I feel as though it is a rite of passage. Jeff and I met at a high school party; he was from another school district but we had mutual friends. It was your typical teenage romance. We spent every available second together, fell in "love" quickly, and we were convinced we were soulmates, even though we barely knew each other. My parents were pretty strict about curfews and where/when I went, but Jeff's family was much more laid back. When my parents' rules were getting in the way of Jeff and I spending time together, we decided to take the leap and move in with each other. This was not thoroughly planned out, since we did not have jobs or a car, but we figured our "love" would make it work!

This began the time period that my parents refer to as the "The Bipolar Train." I was now 18 years old and trying to find myself as a young adult. I felt that my parents' rules were unfair and felt as though I should be allowed to do what I wanted, when I wanted. Jeff shared the same mindset, which only fueled the fire. My parents and I were arguing about things I did and the places I was going, until one night, I decided I had had enough, told Jeff to come pick me up, and packed a bag. When he arrived that night, and my parents saw what was happening, an argument broke out. My mom was begging me to stay, and Jeff and my dad were screaming at each other. Although this was an uncomfortable situation, I truly thought this was what was best for me and, ultimately, for Jeff and me as a couple. We went to Jeff's house with no real plan of how we would survive.

My parents obviously cut me off financially after I moved out, and Jeff had a minimum wage job that obviously could not support us in the long term. One day, my dad reached out to me, asking me to deposit a check my parents had saved for my college. I then did something I never thought I would. I deposited that check into my own bank account, instead of into my parents' account. Yes, that is called stealing, but it was my way of being rebellious. My parents took the money back, and rightfully so.

After we moved in together, Jeff and I quickly realized it was not going to be feasible, long term. One of the major roadblocks we had was, neither one of us had a car (sorry for the pun). Therefore, I moved back in with my parents. Surprisingly, Jeff started to get a bit controlling of me as our relationship went on. He started telling me I had to ask permission before going out with friends.

"Where were you?" Jeff called me, asking one day.

"I went to the library with a friend to study for a biology exam," I replied.

"Well, you didn't ask me if you could go do that," Jeff angrily replied.

"Um, I'm sorry. I didn't know I had to do that, and you were at work, so I had no way of reaching you," I reasoned.

I can't even imagine how terrifying it must have been to find out your girlfriend went to the library!

I found myself apologizing because, clearly, "the love of my life" was always right and he only had my best interest in mind. He was only acting this way because he loved me so much, right? Shortly after this controlling behavior started, I found out that he had hooked up with one of my friends. This crushed me and I began to question our relationship for the first time. His apology for that? He got a tattoo for me, and he told me he would never do it again. In my mind as a young adult, I thought he truly was sorry and we still had a chance at being together forever.

Then the fighting continued. My way of showing Jeff my desperation to make this relationship last was to get a tattoo with his initials in it on my hip. I honestly felt as though he was going to break up with

9

me if I didn't prove my commitment to him. Only four days after I got the tattoo, Jeff and I broke up. Still to this day I am not 100% sure how we broke up. Jeff said he heard from someone I was dating other people, which was absolutely not true.

Oh well, it doesn't really matter now. My tattoo had not even started healing and now the joke was on me. Oh the relief my parents must've felt when we broke up, but that quickly turned to frustration that their daughter would be so naïve as to actually get someone's initials tattooed on her body. Not to forget, they are also not a fan of tattoos. Being the kind, gracious parents they are, they offered to pay to have the tattoo covered up, once it healed.

While waiting for my tattoo to heal, I was healing. This break-up hit me hard and I felt like my life was over. Surely, he was the man I was supposed to marry, and now it was all gone and over. I listened to break-up songs on repeat and cried and cried until there were no more tears left. Even though the relationship was over, he was all I could think about.

One day, I heard a break-up song on the radio and it was as though the words were written from my broken heart. I wrote the lyrics down and sent them to Jeff, hoping maybe he would read them and want to get back together. His response? He told me I wrote a beautiful poem and he would keep it forever. I just didn't have the heart to tell him it was song lyrics and I did not write them myself. Well, I guess he will know the truth now.

Although unbearably painful at times, this break-up was teaching me about relationships and love that would transform me for my future.

No matter how painful it might be, it does not mean it isn't supposed to be happening to you. Yes, it hurts and does not feel right, but it is a part of your journey and is teaching you something. I did some reflecting during this time and realized that when our life changes, we tend to only focus on the "good" of what was before, which causes us to mourn the loss of it. However, if we remember the "bad," it can make the change an opportunity to work out the kinks and be something even better than before!

Hindsight is always 20/20, and what doesn't make sense now will make sense in the future. Just be patient and keep moving forward!

I graduated high school and was off to college, finally. I went off to college and was excited about the endless opportunities that awaited me. Mom and Dad were only an hour away, so that was comforting, but I was far enough away from home to feel as if I was on my own.

I started taking classes and meeting new friends. These new friends had absolutely no clue about the things that had been said about me in middle school. How awesome!

I started off in college as an accounting major since almost all of the "rich" horse families from the barn were accountants. Again, I needed to get a good job so I could afford all the fancy horses. I quickly realized, after starting classes, that accounting was not for me. It was extremely boring and just black and white.

"Dad, I don't like accounting and I don't know what to do with my life, where do I go from here?" I said when I called my dad for guidance.

"You are a people person and creative, I think you should look into human resources," my dad replied.

I took his advice and looked into the world of HR. It was fascinating to me. You get to do so many different things and deal with so many different people. I decided to make the switch in my major and I could not have been happier I did. Human resources was made for me!

College became my new favorite thing. You are living on your own, but Mom and Dad still pay the bills. Don't forget the part of having no curfew. I got to go out on what seemed like a nightly basis with my newfound friends and.... DRINK. (Sorry Mom and Dad, but it is all part of the college experience.)

I met a few different men, none of whom turned out to be anything other than the occasional hangout/kiss at a party type. I still consistently thought about and talked about Jeff, with all the good memories tied to hopes and dreams. I knew the relationship was over, but still had hope that "the one" was out there somewhere. Then I met Greg.

11

From the moment I met Greg, I knew there was something special about him. He was in a fraternity and beamed personality and charm like I had never seen before. We started hanging out at parties at his fraternity's house. He actually lived in the fraternity house in a closet. Yes, you read that correctly. It was undeniable, we had a connection, but there were some red flags. There was excessive drinking, drug use, partying, and even other girls. So much partying, Greg failed out of the university. To be fair to Greg, we were in college and in our early 20s, right? I wasn't exactly innocent here, and I had partaken of my share of fun, but we won't go into that, since my parents are reading this. (Yes, Mom, I was only ever at the library or the chapel.)

Greg and I hung out often and fell in love. Notice the word *love* is not in quotation marks this time, because it was truly love. He was so different than Jeff, and in a good way. This had to be IT... the one God Himself picked out for me to spend the rest of my life with. He got to meet my family, and I met his. His family could almost be considered the exact opposite of mine.

Greg and I had very different families growing up, but we were crazy about each other. His family was always very nice to me, but when Greg would get frustrated with some of his family members, I had trouble relating to the situation. Greg had been through a lot growing up, especially after his dad passed away when he was just a young boy, but it helped him become a strong, independent man. It took him a few months of dating before he felt comfortable enough to tell me about his past, which just shows what a hurtful experience it was for him.

While a significant other's family and upbringing does not define them as a whole, it does contribute to their character and personality. Like I was illustrating in the first chapter, my upbringing and experiences are what made me who I am, and so does yours and everyone else's on this planet.

For example, I watched my parents talk with each other all the time, and they talked with my sister and me about feelings, our day, or we even had a conversation about the weather...this on top of seeing a therapist most of my life.

So what does that mean for me today? I am hard-wired to talk, a lot. I love talking to people about emotions and I feel communication is one of our best tools in relationships. Sorry in advance to my future husband, I'm big on feelings and communication.

Another example is, I grew up watching my parents' marriage. They truly, deeply love each other, and it was so evident to my sister and me. My dad always made my mom his number one priority. At times, it felt as though he put her in front of my sister and me, but that was a beautiful thing. He cared for her well-being, and still does to this day. Don't be mistaken, their marriage wasn't perfect, I can recall several "rough patches" when they could be heard yelling at each other after the kids went to bed. There was a time the arguing was so frequent, I feared they would get divorced. Fortunately, they worked through it, and I would later find out that my mom had put her foot down and demanded my dad go to therapy or else she was done. What was his response? You guessed it, he did anything and everything she asked and set out to fight for their marriage.

Holy smokes! That is powerful. We all know no marriage is perfect and see the divorce rate climb every year, but it takes hard work from both people to figure out the way to make it work. On your wedding day, you are promising to do whatever it takes to make things work. They should really consider updating the vows recited at a wedding ceremony. But I'm no expert on marriage, as we will see later.

Now, let me make this clear: Just because a person has a bad upbringing, such as abuse or neglect, does not mean they will be predestined to re-create that in their own families. Sometimes it happens, but not all the time. I've met many people who have had less than ideal families, but they turned out to be wonderful human beings. It is based on the person's perspective of their situation. Do they take their situation as an example of what to do, or an example of what not to do? We are not in control of the families or experiences we have in life, but we are in control of how we react.

Make sense? We will look into this concept later, stay tuned.

Back to Greg and me. We were following the normal path of any adult relationship you expect to see nowadays. Well, maybe it was a tad different than an adult relationship. In our story there was drinking, and lots of it. We were crazy about each other, but the heavy drinking often turned into fights, big ones, mostly because I would bring up insecurities I had from my relationship with Jeff. Pile that on top of drinking that makes you think and speak irrationally. Boom! There were fights. I am embarrassed by many of the fights I started, but it was college.

We had lots of fun and were making many memories together, Greg and I. Once, I remember we were walking back to the dorm after a party. While on our walk back, someone ran a red light and hit Greg with their car.

"Greg! Are you ok?!" I asked, frightened.

"Yeah, but where are my shoes?" Greg replied in a raspy voice.

The person who hit him with their car just drove off! Fortunately, we found his shoes and hitched a ride to the hospital with a witness of the accident; we had Greg checked out at the local hospital and everything was ok. Since we had no car, we had to walk back to campus from the hospital and it was pouring rain. Being a social media fanatic, I posted a status that we were walking home from the hospital in the rain and forgot that my mom would see this status. I suffered the consequences for my action when my mother frantically called me the next morning.

So, as you can see, I was your typical college student. I enjoyed going to parties with friends, but I also enjoyed going home on some weekends for my mom to do my laundry and I could catch up on the one thing I wasn't doing at college, sleep!

I had a boyfriend, yes, and he was great, but it was yet another "young love" to add to my life.

What is young love? To me, it is that love when you find somebody you don't hate and you actually like to be around them. They are amusing and fun. They genuinely want to be around you, too. Now I am not saying that you don't love each other, because you certainly do, however, it is a love that lives on the surface of your heart. So does that mean all young love eventually ends? Not at all, my dear. Every kind of love starts out as young love. Then, as you grow together and evolve as people, it breaks through the surface and turns into that grow-old-together love. Not all young love turns into that, as you can see what happened to Jeff and me.

Greg and I were on the path to be breaking the surface of that young love stage and into the Notebook type love. Will it work out? Only time will tell, stay tuned!

Mom Here

This one is going to be raw

I have to share a few things about the Jeff period. It was one of the hardest times of my life. I feel the need to share some of the details, as I am positive there are many out there who have experienced, or are experiencing a surreal time in their lives. So Heather, buckle your seat belt because, I believe, you are not even aware of some of this.

Heather meets Jeff and shortly thereafter turns 18. As my husband aptly calls it, "The Bipolar Train Period." It was as if this young woman I had known got on the train and left. She began to say things like, "I don't feel like I belong in this family;" "I am an adult and can do whatever I want;" "I don't have to listen to you." Then there was the evening she came home past curfew, and while we were talking, I saw the first tattoo on the inside of her left wrist. A Chinese symbol for inner strength. That will actually become very significant a few years later. Little did I know it was only just the start of the surreal period.

A few weeks later, Jeff shows up at our house late one night and Heather states she is leaving and going to live with him. There was yelling, my husband in a T-shirt and underwear in our front yard begging Heather not to leave, and a physical altercation about to break out between my husband and Jeff. Thankfully, clearer minds prevailed and there were no physical punches thrown. As you already know, Heather left. I could not believe what had just happened. I was unable to breathe I was so upset. I almost made a trip to the emergency room, but was able to calm myself.

Heather was gone for two weeks, during which time I really wasn't sure where she was. As a mom, that was devastating. Through a friend of hers, I did know she was still attending school, thank you, Lord, for that. I also heard they were planning on getting food stamps

15

and going to the food bank for food. We made a difficult decision, that if this is what she wanted, we were not going to support any of it. To recognize your daughter has made a foolish decision, and to practice hard love by cutting off any support, was the most difficult decision I ever made. I remember her sister calling me and saying she met Heather at a store and asking if she could buy her a soda, and I said no. Then there was an instance when Heather tried to get the money we had set aside for college, because it was in her name at the bank. My heart was not only broken, but shattered.

We met with Heather, Jeff, and his mother and talked about the situation. We just wanted her to get an education. If she decided that he was the one, that was great, but please come home and go to college. She did and it was a rough beginning, but we all worked at rebuilding our relationship. I was still harboring some anger and hurt that she had done this. I had prayed and prayed, but was not sure what to do with those emotions. My older daughter suggested writing her a letter I would never send. I did, and it was filled with anger, some language I never use, and tear stained in many places. It was so cathartic to release those emotions. It then went quickly into the fireplace. I strongly recommend this technique to help put past hurts aside.

Lastly, we all were able to move forward with lessons that we did not realize would come in handy in the not-too-distant future.

The time came for Heather to start her next adventure, college. I was so very excited for her. College would be a wonderful place for her to grow, learn, and I am not naïve, party. It was very quiet in our house after she left, but I knew she was not far away. About two weeks into her college experience, my phone rings about 1a.m., and when I answered, all I heard were guys' voices and a lot of laughter. I could tell there was a party at hand. I kept saying Heather's name but with no response. Of course, it was just an accidental call, but I had images of her being taken advantage of and I had no way of reaching her. Please give me grace! 1a.m., phone rings and daughter is away at college. Thank you, Lord, it was an accidental call.

Just one more note about the night Greg was hit by the car. Social media is at play here. I see a post from my daughter stating it is 3 a.m. and she is walking home from the emergency room in the rain. When

I try to call her to make sure she is OK, she doesn't answer her phone. Another gray hair, thank you Heather!

Our children are going to want to grow up faster than we know is safe. There will be times, and honestly still are, that I would have made a different decision, but God gave us free will. Sometimes we need the good, bad, and ugly experiences to shape us into the people He wants us to become. Just try to love them through it!

Dad Here

Remember being heartbroken, confused and frustrated. My little girl, my baby, left our loving home for a boy. I had always warned both daughters, "Boys are bad. I know I was one."

Questioning where did I go wrong? What can I do? God told me to continue to always love her, to surrender the circumstances all to Him, and within a couple of days, she was back home.

When Heather went off to college, I was very happy for her. I felt she was ready to experience life on her own, yet knowing that we were still there for her and supporting her. I loved college and wanted the same for her, to take this opportunity to figure out where her desires and energy would lead her.

The Big Debut

I was just bopping around through life. I was going to school full time, dating my boyfriend, horseback riding, and just being your typical young 20-something-year-old. But things were about to take an interesting turn. Sound fun? Well, it was not fun for me.

I was home for Christmas break, and one morning Greg and I were driving to go pick up my mom from work. Just a status quo morning, and I was driving the car. I can still feel what comes next.

I am driving along the highway and, all of a sudden, it was like a wave of brain fog came over me and I felt extremely fatigued. I remember telling Greg, "Wow, I just got really tired all of a sudden. That's weird!" I continued driving the car and we picked up my mom at her office.

On the way home, my mom wanted to stop at the grocery to pick up some things. I remember how overwhelming it was being in the grocery store. It is hard to explain, but it was as if my brain could not process all the stimuli found in a grocery store. All the people, lights, and food items were just too much to handle, and gave me a headache.

"Mom, my head feels weird, I have lots of pressure," I cried to my mom.

"Oh honey, here is some Advil™. When we get home, you can take a nap and feel better," my mom said, as she put the car in reverse to head home.

When I awoke from my nap, I felt a little better, but now my tongue felt different. I know, that is a weird thing to say, but it is true. My tongue felt like pins and needles.

"Mom, now my tongue feels like pins and needles," I said anxiously.

"You probably just burnt it on coffee this morning," my mom reasoned.

I was feeling as though she wasn't taking me seriously. I had flashbacks to when I was in school and would say my stomach hurt, but she still put my behind on that school bus and told me to suck it up. I'll be honest, I was faking my symptoms back then, but I definitely wasn't faking it this time.

After going to bed early, I woke up in the middle of the night. I quickly noticed something was definitely wrong and it was not a migraine. I could now feel it down the entire left side of my body. You know the feeling you get when your foot falls "asleep?" That horrible pins and needles stabbing you? Well, I had that feeling down my entire left side. You got that right; this was not normal. I went into my parents' bedroom and woke my mom, telling her about my newly-revealed symptoms. She told me to go back to bed and we would see how I felt in the morning.

I finally put an end to her shrugging off my symptoms and said no. I pleaded with her that I truly felt something was seriously not right and I needed to go to the hospital.

We went to the hospital where they did a scan of my brain since I was displaying some symptoms associated with a stroke. I remember not feeling panicked, as one would expect to feel, because certainly, this was not a stroke. Well, I was wrong about that one!

The doctor came in with the results of my scan and said they found blood in my brain and were discussing life-flying me by helicopter to another hospital that was better equipped to handle this type of medical emergency.

Okay, the panic started to seep in now. *How could a healthy 22-year-old be having a stroke?* That is what the doctors at the next hospital would be pressed to figure out.

Since I was stable, they took me to the neighboring hospital by ambulance instead of a helicopter. That was a bummer, because being flown in a helicopter would have been a much cooler story to tell. But

I am sure this was a far less dramatic way to transport me, as well as slightly reassuring that I wasn't on the verge of death. But I was still scared and could not think of any possible reason my brain was bleeding. I am no doctor, but I do know enough to know that your brain isn't supposed to bleed. Not good.

When I arrived at the second hospital, they rushed me into the operating room to perform a procedure called an angiogram. This procedure was to see if I was having a brain aneurysm. The nurse was prepping me for the procedure and she commented on how she liked the tattoo I had. This was the tattoo I had covering up the one I got for Jeff. I did not feel this was the time to go into the backstory, nor did I have the energy to do so. I just gave her a simple, "Thank you." This nurse was about to be helping me during a very important procedure; I didn't want her questioning my life choices!

For this procedure, they insert a tube through the femoral artery in your groin area and then push it up to your brain to shoot a dye. Now picture the distance from your groin to your brain... pretty far distance? Yes, and it hurt as much as you would think it would. They gave me morphine while I was shouting out in pain, which definitely helped, but I wish they had put me to sleep for this. Since that wasn't an option, I just closed my eyes and pictured myself in Aruba. I am sure the morphine helped me on this trip.

The angiogram showed I was not having a brain aneurysm, which would have meant sending me off to emergency brain surgery. Although, they still did not know where this blood came from, they sent me off for an extensive brain MRI.

If you have ever had an MRI before, you will appreciate how incredibly loud they are. Like, deafening loud. Just a bunch of banging around while you lay in a tube. Thank God I am not claustrophobic! Halfway through the MRI, I hear a voice on the loud speaker "Hey! You have to stay awake. You fell asleep and moved, so now we have to start over," the angry nurse yelled. All I could think was, maybe they shouldn't have given me so much morphine if they wanted me to stay awake! I just focused on staying awake for the rest of the test. I focused on the banging noises and imagined words being said instead. It is actually quite entertaining to do that while getting an MRI, find words that matched the tones and inflections. I use this trick still today when getting tests done.

The MRI of my brain showed I had a lesion called a *Cavernous Malformation* in my brain that had bled.

What the heck is that?

I was right there with you, I had absolutely no idea what that was. So, I did what any 21st Century person would do... I googled it!

There wasn't much to find on the internet other than a definition of a Cavernous Malformation: A **cavernous malformation** (also called a cavernoma, **cavernous** angioma, or a "cav-mal"), is a rare type of vascular **malformation**, meaning an abnormality of the blood vessels. A "cav-mal" can occur in any part of the body, but it's usually only a threat in the brain or spinal cord. Great, it's rare and not much information to be given on the internet. Before discharging me, the hospital set up an appointment for me with a neurosurgeon.

I had a long list of questions written down to ask the neurosurgeon at my first appointment and it went like this:

ME: Why is my brain bleeding, Doc?

Neurosurgeon: You have a Cavernoma on your right thalamus. It is made up of very weak blood vessels which can rupture or leak, causing blood in your brain. Your lesion leaked a little bit of blood, which caused your symptoms leading you to the hospital.

ME: How did it get there?

Neurosurgeon: From what we understand, you were most likely born with it, but it has remained dormant all these years.

ME: Well, what are we going to do about it?

Neurosurgeon: Since this condition is rare, there is no current known treatment, and the only cure is brain surgery to remove the lesion.

ME: Brain surgery is scary, but I don't want this thing bleeding again, so sign me up!

21

Neurosurgeon: Unfortunately, your lesion is in a very delicate part of the brain. If this was a game of Monopoly©, it would be called Park Place. Your lesion is in a part of your brain that controls major body functions. Cavernomas usually do not bleed that frequently, and you could live the rest of your life and it would never cause another problem. Since the risks of brain surgery outweigh the benefits of brain surgery, we are going to just watch it and wait.

ME: What can I do to decrease the chances of it bleeding again?

Neurosurgeon: We really don't fully understand what causes these lesions to bleed, but you could try and avoid blood thinners to be extra cautious.

ME: No blood thinners, check! Anything else I can do?

Neurosurgeon: Not really, just live your life!

ME: Last question, can I drink Jager Bomb shots? Those are my favorite!

Neurosurgeon: I don't think so; those aren't a good idea even for people without Cavernomas!

Okay, so I have this thing in my brain that just bled, is considered inoperable, and there's nothing I can really do to prevent it from bleeding again? Well, that is just plain terrifying! At no fault of the doctor, I left the appointment feeling very overwhelmed. It felt as though I had a ticking time bomb in my head, and my health/life was out of my control. I'll admit, I am a bit of a control freak. But this was now something absolutely 100% out of my control. I was supposed to go "live my life" as if I didn't have a lesion in my brain that could rupture at any given moment.

This was what I like to call, "a world stopper." Never in my life would I have guessed I would get a diagnosis such as this. This clearly was going to change the rest of my life, and the scary part was, there was no way of knowing the extent of the change. All we knew was right now. What we know right now was, I have an inoperable lesion in my brain that could or could not bleed again.

I was absolutely terrified and felt as though my life was over. I remember having nightmares that would wake me up in a cold sweat at night. In these horrifying dreams, I was pulling up to a funeral home and my family was standing outside, sobbing uncontrollably. I walk up the stairs and open the big oak doors to an empty room. I walk inside and follow the signs with arrows guiding me to the back of the building. Then I entered a room in the back, which was filled with empty chairs and tissues crumbled up on the floor. Up against the far wall there is a casket with Greg kneeling in front of it and praying. I yell out his name but he does not seem to hear me so I walk towards him. As I approach him, I see the face of the person lying in the casket. You guessed it... it's me. I look no older than 25 years old. Terrifying, I know.

That should give you a pretty good picture of how scared I was. Growing up, when I was sick, I would go to the doctor and he would give me medicine and make me all better. This was not the case this time. There wasn't any medicine the doctor could give me to make me better. As we all come to learn in our lives, childhood is a lot simpler than adulthood. My life had taken an unexpected turn and I was not sure how to handle the turbulence.

What I learned here was, we are constantly learning about ourselves. This was a learning experience for me by recognizing my wanting to control everything about my life, but that is just not possible in every situation. My brain, my health, was now out of my hands. What could I do about that? Well, I could either let the anxiety and fear make me miserable and psychologically sick, or I could give this to God, who is the One who actually is in control of everything. I can assure you, the pain we face, the struggles we deal with, are all going to make sense one day. I know it can be oh so difficult to see that in the midst of the storm, but you are stronger than you think. I was initially irritated by the doctor's words, "Just live your life," because I felt like that was impossible and there is no way he understood what this was like. But in reality, that was the best advice he could've given me. I couldn't control my diagnosis and the fact it was "incurable," but what I could control was how I responded to it.

Therefore, I did just that. I was a full-time college student, still enjoying my time with Greg, and watching our relationship grow. I was still riding horses, and hanging out with friends. Horseback riding was my escape. When I was on my horse, there was no focus on the medical diagnosis I had, my only focus was on how to ride and it was quite refreshing. When I was in normal day-to-day life, I was worried about every headache or weird feeling I got. Was it another brain bleed? It's not like a little bell would go off when it happens to signal I was having another hemorrhage. They really should create an app for that!

After my diagnosis, I did make a promise to myself to focus on my health more. I couldn't do anything about my brain issue, but I could make sure the rest of my body was as healthy as could be. So, I took up running. It was very hard at first, but I quickly learned how much of an escape running was when I was up at college and could not ride my horse who was back home. Not to forget, running was an excellent way to lose weight! The pounds just fell off me, and for the first time in my life, I felt so confident in my own skin. Have you heard of that "runner's high" people talk about? Well, I can assure you, it's totally a real thing!

Despite what my brain was doing, I felt absolutely fantastic. Greg and I were getting more and more serious by the day, he enrolled in a community college, and I felt like things were looking up. Little did I know, things would have to get worse before they got better.

Mom Here

Do you all remember when Heather said in Chapter 1 that I was very bright with the whole potty thing and I said not so much, given I was putting my two-year-old on the back of a pony? Well, here is more proof. I gave my daughter Advil, a blood thinner, when her brain was bleeding. Oh, and it gets better. I did not recognize the symptoms of a stroke, even though my professional career involved working at a rehabilitation facility with folks who had suffered strokes and spinal cord injuries. Yup, way to go Mom!

I knew something was wrong when we were in the ER. After Heather's CT scans, the nurse never left the room. That never happens. My family has always dealt with life emergencies by cracking jokes and keeping the mood light as possible. So, as we were waiting for the doctor to decide how to transport her, I reminded Heather of

24

the time we were here after she had fallen off a horse. They decided to send her to Children's Hospital, and the ambulance drivers came, loaded her on a gurney, forgot to lock it, and almost dropped her. However, that was not the only adventure that day. On our way to Children's Hospital, we were stopped at an intersection and someone was speeding through it and hit a telephone pole right in front of us.

The paramedic said, "I have to check to make sure they are OK until another ambulance can come."

I said, "Well do what you need to."

No sooner had I said that but the driver of the car jumped out and ran away! When we arrived at Children's Hospital, 10 people came running at us, just like in the movies, and said, "Are you the girl that was on the way to the hospital when the ambulance got in an accident?"

Just as I finished the story on this day of her brain hemorrhage, who walked in the room to transport Heather? That same paramedic from years ago! She said she had just finished telling her partner that story.

I drove separately to the hospital and was directed up to an inpatient room. I remember sitting there looking out the window in shock and frightened. This was never on my Mom radar. Drinking, drugs, boys, yes. But a brain bleed at 22, no. This was my baby girl, the one who had righted her life, and was doing so beautifully in school, and had such a bright future. What did this mean? What would the future hold for all of us? When a child is sick, you want nothing more than to make them feel better. Usually, you can, by taking them to the doctor, giving them medicine, and hugs and kisses. That was not going to work in this situation. As I would quickly come to realize there were even more questions than answers in the medical community about this diagnosis.

I needed answers!

I began to pray, google, and reach out to the physiatrist I had worked with at the rehab facility. I did find an organization called Angioma Alliance that was started by a Mom whose daughter was diagnosed with this rare brain condition, but more on that later. So, I was taking what action I could, determined to learn as much about this as possible.

However, information did not change the fact that my daughter had a life-threatening medical condition, one that I could personally do nothing about, and I might lose her. I could not imagine how I would navigate that one.

At this moment, I realized life takes us places that we never expect. I guess, as the saying goes, we have to expect the unexpected. All of us have different ways to deal with that. For me, it is God, learning as much as I can, and reaching out for support of others. That is partially what this book is about. Whether it be brain bleeds, or a tough season of parenting, help is out there.

Dad Here

All I could think about then was, "Life is good." We had recently returned from Thanksgiving in Aruba, one daughter out of college, and Heather close to being done (No more tuition in sight). Our marketing business was doing well, I was just honored to be asked to be President of the Pittsburgh Chapter of EO (which is an international Entrepreneurial Organization).

Like Heather, I have trusted the medical community to diagnose the problem and fix it, via medicine or whatever means they felt appropriate. Unfortunately, this time they were stumped about what they could or should do to help my baby. I am a dad, we fix things. I truly felt helpless at this point. Ok, we have a big challenge here; we need a strategy and a plan to overcome this obstacle. I'll reach out to the International Entrepreneurial Organization (EO) and see if they have any connections or contacts that can help. They did, and helped us get in touch with other brain surgeons. I will do anything to help my baby get better. We will get through this together.

The Puzzle

I hate puzzles. My mom loves them, but I find them very stressful. You have to sort through all these pieces and figure out where they belong. I just don't enjoy that at all. Well, my life had suddenly turned into one giant puzzle, or so it felt. After receiving my medical diagnosis of Cavernous Angioma, I did as much research as possible, since my neurosurgeon appointment left me feeling hopeless.

On my quest to find some hope, I did find an organization called Angioma Alliance. It was a group/community full of people from around the world who had the same diagnosis. I wasn't alone! In this community, I got to talk with people and hear about their own personal experiences with this disease. It is a wonderful place to ask questions and, at times, just vent on how unfair this is.

I also gained information on neurosurgeons around the country who specialize in Cavernous Angioma and are willing to look at your brain scans and give you second opinions. Can't hurt, right?

So I did just that, I sent my scans to a couple different neurosurgeons. There were three main neurosurgeons named to specialize in this disease: One was in Arizona, one was in California, and one was in Chicago. We sent my scans to these top neurosurgeons and eagerly waited for their responses to viewing them. I shouldn't say, "we." I was away at college and my mom orchestrated all of this. *Thanks, Mom!*

My parents and I decided to drive to Chicago to meet with the top neurosurgeon who was recommended by Angioma Alliance. I remember being so nervous and hopeful at the same time, nervous that he would say the same thing as the neurosurgeon I saw already, and hopeful there was a chance he might have something else to say. I mean, he specializes in these little demons; he must know of a treatment we could try to prevent it from bleeding again.

I won't keep you in suspense... he did not have anything else to say. He agreed my lesion was too deep in my brain to operate. Brain surgery would most likely paralyze my left side, and chances were, this may not ever bleed again. I was so frustrated. He was very nice and definitely knowledgeable about angiomas, but he did not give me the answer I would have loved to hear, "Heather, take this pill and it will magically make the Cavernous Angioma disappear!"

Even though he did not give me the answer that could make this all go away, I had hope...hope that maybe these other neurosurgeons to whom we had sent my scans would have a solution. Meanwhile, I did make a follow-up appointment with the Chicago doctor in a few months, to see how things were going and get a follow up brain scan to see if there were any changes.

I just continued living my life. I was a full-time college student and running almost every day. I quickly was in the best shape of my life, feeling confident in how I looked and felt. One of the best things you can do for yourself in a time of anxiety is find healthy outlets for your pain and suffering. Obviously drinking or doing drugs is not the answer. What I mean here is something that you enjoy that could provide you with an escape from reality and make you healthier! These things vary from person to person but could be exercise, reading books, volunteer work, playing a musical instrument, or spending time with family and friends. Sometimes you may have a couple different outlets, like for me it was running and riding my horse.

I got the second opinions from the neurosurgeons from Arizona and California. Both suggested they do the brain surgery to remove my lesion. Well, that complicated things. Every neurosurgeon I had seen in person said it was too deep and inoperable. They indicated that the risks of surgery far outweighed the benefits, but now I had two doctors saying they could do it, and have done it in the past, to other people with similar situations. So, what do I do? This seemed to be a gamble, no matter what decision I made.

This was so conflicting and hard for me. Do I go ahead and let one of these two neurosurgeons cut into my brain and remove this thing?

Or do I follow the direction of the other neurosurgeons and just let it be and live my life? This was the hardest decision of my life. If I decided to have the brain surgery one of two things could happen:

Scenario One: The surgeon successfully removes the lesion. After a couple weeks, I am feeling great, out riding my horse, and living my life without this bleeding time bomb in my head anymore!

Scenario Two: While in surgery, the lesion ruptures and I have a massive stroke, either permanently paralyzing me or killing me.

If I decided to not have the brain surgery one of two things could happen.

Scenario One - A: I live my life and this lesion never bleeds again... EVER!

Scenario Two - A: Out of nowhere, I have another bleed that paralyzes me for the rest of my life or kills me.

See how hard this was? Both options had potential, immense risks, and both had chances to be very successful. How does a person choose between two potential death sentences? This was too big of a decision for a 22-year-old to make. The only decisions I should have been making right then were what color dress to wear to my sorority formal dance! But this was my reality and I had to face it.

When life takes a turn and you feel like there is no hope, the best thing to do is just accept the reality. At first, it feels like a dream... well, more like a nightmare, but once we change our focus and accept that this is what life has dealt us, it becomes more manageable. We don't have to accept the level of fairness or unfairness, but if you just accept the fact that this is your reality, or journey, then it can change your perspective. That is exactly what I did in order to make a decision that had the potential to change the rest of my life. Or potentially end it.

I did a lot of research, mostly through Angioma Alliance, and talking with my family. Greg was also present to help be my sounding bar of options. After lots of prayer and research, I decided to not have the surgery and take the more conservative route of hoping it doesn't bleed again. The only two doctors who were recommending surgery were the only two who had not seen me in person, only saw my brain scans. They could not see how well I was doing. I was living my life!

Then, one day, I was watching television, and all of a sudden, a wave of exhaustion came over me. Much like that time I was in the car with Greg a few months before, although something else was different: My vision was blurry. I called the first person that came to mind, my mom. We discussed my symptoms and were discussing whether or not I was having another brain bleed. I decided not to go to the hospital because my vision problems quickly subsided and I had my follow-up appointment with the Chicago doctor soon. It was a very scary and hard decision, but I did the only thing I knew would take my mind off my symptoms and fear of another hemorrhage, I went riding.

While riding my horse that afternoon, I noticed I was having trouble focusing and not being able to control my horse the way I was supposed to. While still in the saddle, I broke down crying. I was so upset that my brain "problems" were affecting my riding. Riding was the thing I used to escape from my reality, remember? So, I was determined to overcome my symptoms and not give up on my ride.

I kept riding that day and while trying to jump some fences, I made a riding error, which resulted in me falling off my horse. Luckily, I was only slightly injured by my fall, a twisted ankle, but my self-esteem was hurt the most. Certainly, this demon in my brain could not interfere with my riding. Not fair!

Then came my follow-up appointment in Chicago. The doctor ordered a new brain scan before my appointment and that showed what I was most fearful of... another brain bleed. Chicago Neurosurgeon explained, since it had bled again in only six months' time from the first one, it was time to talk about our options. He recommended a procedure called Gamma Knife surgery. This is where they shoot localized radiation into the angioma in the hopes it will harden the blood vessels that keep leaking blood.

The catch? It takes about two years after the procedure to take effect. Oh, and they are not 100% sure it works for angiomas, yet. Not very comforting! I told him I would need to think about it before committing.

I immediately reached out to people in the Angioma Alliance group to see if they had Gamma Knife and could tell me their own experiences. The responses were mixed; some people said they believed Gamma Knife caused more brain bleeds, and a couple people had success with it. Since it was my only option at this point, I decided to just go for it!

The Chicago doctor recommended a doctor in my hometown that was an expert with Gamma Knife. I went with that referral, because if anyone was going to be messing with my brain, I wanted it to be an expert! I prayed so much before making this decision, and I can truly say I believe God led me to decide to have the procedure. And it is always good manners to listen to The Man Upstairs!

I had the Gamma Knife surgery on a Friday, and was sent home the same day. My parents and I joked about this, since it was like outpatient brain surgery, and maybe one day they will have a drive through brain surgery!

Since this procedure would hopefully harden, or rust my leaky blood vessels in my brain, we were using, "Rust Heather," as our new mantra. Maybe my brain was already rusting, because I went home after the procedure with a massive headache!

I had another bleed a month after the Gamma Knife. We have no idea if the procedure caused it, or it was just the nature of my angioma itself. But once again, I recovered pretty quickly and went back to living my life.

Was I scared it kept bleeding? Absolutely. However, I did not let that fear consume me. I accepted the fact I had zero control over what was happening in my brain, and just put my focus on living my best life, which was something I *could* control.

Isn't that true with any hardship or situation in which we find ourselves? We can only control our reactions to certain situations. You are most certainly allowed to feel scared and anxious over things over which you have no control but try and fight that anxiety with a positive and assured attitude.

I had this uncontrollable bleeding thing in my brain, but I was trying my hardest not to let it control my entire life. Easier said than done, right?

31

There were so many false alarms along the way, too many false alarms to count. There were days I would get a headache and rush to the emergency room thinking it could be another bleed. Then tests showed it was nothing and they sent me home. These false alarms made me feel humiliated and stupid. I had to remind myself that it is not as though a bell would go off each time my brain started bleeding again. Wouldn't that be something!

Then my life took another turn, however, this was a happier turn. Finally! It was a fall weekend here in South Western Pennsylvania and Greg and I were away with my parents at the summer place Greg's family owned. We had invited my parents for the weekend to relax and enjoy the fall weather by the lake. Greg and I had gotten in a pretty big fight on the way to the lake house from a binge-drinking event Greg had partaken in the night before.

During this argument in the car I told him, "I am really glad we aren't engaged right now because I don't know if I want to marry you!" Ouch.

Greg decided to change the water filter right before my family arrived and somehow managed to shut off all the water to the house. We had no running water for the first 24 hours of our family fun weekend. Going outside to go to the bathroom and washing up in a gas station bathroom sink were new experiences I never thought I'd have with my family, but it was an adventure! Greg planned a nice dinner for us all at a restaurant nestled on the lake. Greg was noticeably very nervous at dinner, even spilling his soup in his lap.

Remember the big fight we had on our way to the lake? This did not deter Greg, and he proposed at dinner. I said yes and immediately broke down sobbing afterwards. Were these tears of hesitation or tears of joy? I was not clear about it then, but I am now. More on this later.

Mom Here-

I do like puzzles and, with my past professional career in the medical field, I put my emotions aside and began to find out as much as possible about this disease. I suppose that is how I deal with stressful situations. Luckily, Google™ had been created and that is how I found the Angioma Alliance. It was started by Connie Lee, PsyD, President and CEO. In January of 2000, her then four-month-old daughter Julia received brain surgery for a major brain hemorrhage caused by a Cavernous Angioma. Julia has the genetic kind of the disease, so she actually has multiple angiomas. Connie has created an organization that not only provides information to people, but also has spearheaded research for a cure other than brain surgery.

I found out that 1 in 500 people have a cavernous angioma, but only one percent of them bleed. I knew she was special. As Heather mentioned, hers was in not only the deepest part of her brain, but essentially what they call the control center. Most activities filter through the thalamus before our body takes action. So here we were, with an inoperable bleeding angioma that none of us could do anything about. A blessing we later learned was that she did not have the hereditary form, but the sporadic gene, so just one angioma, but a dangerous one.

My daughter continued to live her life with courage and grace that I found hard to understand. Remember that tattoo I saw on her left wrist when she came home after curfew? Chinese symbol for Inner Strength. Who knew?

I have to share a little story about the weekend at the lake. As Heather said, we headed up for a fun weekend. Greg and Heather arrived before us and Greg changed the water filter, as it was well water and had an odor. Well, poor guy, put it in incorrectly and couldn't remove it. So future in-laws are on their way and no water, plus his girlfriend has just said she is glad they are not engaged. It gets better.

It is pouring down rain all weekend and the plumber can't get there till Sunday. So, to answer nature's call, we have to go outside in the rain and do nature's business. Oh, and there is more, we have to get ready for the big dinner where the proposal is happening, so we head on over to Walmart™ to go into their bathrooms to wash up. Never expected to say I did that. Fast forward to dinner. Greg is very nervous, spills his soup all over the table, but pushes forward and asks Heather the big question. She says yes and then 20 minutes later, Heather asks me to get out of the car with her and is crying hysterically. Poor Greg is sitting in the car, thinking, "This was not how I saw this weekend going."

All in all, it was a fun weekend with many laughs which we needed at the time.

I so appreciate the forethought and initiative Connie Lee took in starting Angioma Alliance. Here she was, a new mom with a four-month-old daughter who had a rare medical condition. Rather than throw up her hands and do nothing, she took action, starting a site to share information worldwide. With committed effort, not only has it done that, but it also has spearheaded research, and currently drug trials for treatment, instead of just brain surgery. I hope we all look forward to solutions and not just stay stuck when life sends a storm our way!

Dad Here

I don't care for puzzles either, but I do thrive on challenges and creatively coming up with solutions. Unfortunately, this was not that type of challenge.

So many times, I would see in many of the assorted doctors' faces that they were puzzled about what this was, and how to best treat it. As the Dad, I just wanted to fix it and let Heather get along with her very promising life.

I thought a doctor in Chicago, in whom I had very high hopes because of his experience and reputation, would know. He is a world-renowned brain surgeon. His closing comment to us was, "Everyone has their demons."

Is Heather possessed? Do we need to get a priest?

As we drove seven hours back to Pittsburgh, I kept watching for Heather's head to twirl around 360 degrees. Then I realized he was referring to everyone and their problems and life challenges. I believe it was his way of saying, "It's going to be ok."

At this point, Heather is 22 years old, these are her decisions, it is her life. All I could do was listen to her explain what she was thinking, while I was feeling and praying very hard for God to guide her decisions and give her peace.

My initial thoughts on Gamma Knife was, "You are going to do what? In hopes of what? And it's going to take how long before we know if it is actually going to work?" All I can say is, I was glad I didn't have to make that decision.

The Chaos

We all have that picture of how our life will turn out, right? It is more or less a plan we make, a plan filled with hopes and dreams. What was mine? Well, I graduate college with a degree and start a fancy career in which I make loads of money and have a fancy car, just so everyone who sees me knows I am successful. Not to forget, I get married to this amazing man and we have the most beautiful children. In my spare time, you can find me at the barn, riding my very fancy horse and getting ready for the next big competition. Life is good.

Then, here comes the reality. News flash, life does not always go as planned. I certainly was no exception.

In my reality, I am newly engaged and in the best shape of my life (thanks to running and a healthy diet) and a full time junior in college. Life is great, right? Yes, and no.

Sure, my life has a lot of positives and things to look forward to, but let's not forget this uncontrollable bleeding demon in my brain! I sure could not forget its existence, but I really was trying to do my best and be optimistic. God had led me to the decision to get the Gamma Knife, and now I must have faith and wait for it to work. It had already bled again since the Gamma Knife, but surely that was just a fluke; now things will be smooth sailing from here on out. I was very wrong.

Just two weeks after the third brain hemorrhage, a fourth struck my reality. It was not anything major to warrant surgery, but it was enough to shake my confidence and see another neurosurgeon. This one was the Chief of Neurosurgery at the hospital in my hometown, University of Pittsburgh Medical Center, or UPMC. He was in agreement with the other neurosurgeons I had encountered; my lesion was inoperable. This statement had become so common to me that it no longer affected me like it had in the beginning. I think it showed how I had truly accepted my diagnosis and come to terms with it. I have this abnormal thing in my brain, but it is going to stay there and this is my "new normal." I was not accepting the unfairness of my situation, but I could accept its reality.

My diagnosis and lack of treatment options sucked. It was totally unfair. I was so angry at how my body could fail me like this, and angry at the medical professionals. Isn't it their job to find a solution to your problem? If I get a sinus infection, they give me antibiotics and I get better. Pretty easy, huh? I even jokingly questioned my own mother whether she did drugs while I was in her womb and that may have caused this abnormal growth in my brain. She assured me she followed the pregnancy guidelines impeccably and had zero contributions to my bleeding brain.

So here I was, having to accept the fact I just had horrendous bad luck. But if I let it consume me and define me as a person, then I would be giving it more power. Yes, that is easier said than done, but hear me out.

We are only defined by our reactions to things. If someone finds a homeless dog, rescues it, and provides a loving home to that animal, you would view that person in a different light than you would a person who finds a homeless dog, does nothing with the poor animal, and just leaves it starving out in the cold.

What do those two people have in common? They both found a homeless dog. What is the difference in the outcomes of your perspective of these people? It was all defined by their individual reactions to finding the dog. How did two people respond to the same situation?

What I learned here was, our lives are defined by our own personal reactions to situations. Whether our reactions are intentional or not, they are what makes us who we are and how the world views us. Lucky for us, our reactions to situations are about the only thing we can control. Life happens. We have absolutely no control over it. We must try and accept that fact. The only thing we can control is our reaction to when life happens. It's not always easy.

37

I was struggling with what was happening in my life. I was allowing the unfairness of my situation to infiltrate my brain with negative thoughts and feelings of helplessness. In addition, I was immensely struggling with my faith in God. He had led me to my decision of Gamma Knife, and now my brain continues to keep bleeding. I know He is able to create miracles and heal people, but where is He now?

I had never felt so distant from God before in my entire life. I felt as if He was silent, or ignoring me, or maybe He didn't exist at all? Certainly, if He does exist, He would perform a miracle and zap this thing out of my brain!

Then there was my engagement. Yes, it was exciting to plan a wedding, but my health issues and fear of my future were overshadowing things. Would I even be alive for my wedding? Would I be in a wheelchair and unable to walk down the aisle? Greg didn't seem too worried, and I was thankful for that. Well, maybe he was and just kept it to himself.

I was in a dark place. I not only was questioning my faith in God, but I was also questioning my faith in my decision-making skills and in myself. Why didn't I just have the brain surgery in Arizona or California? I potentially could have had the brain surgery in Arizona or California, had my lesion removed successfully, encountered zero deficits, and got back on track for my "plan" of my life.

However, here I am in my reality, having tried the Gamma Knife, and it does not seem to be working, my faith is diminishing, and my hope of a bright future is as good as gone.

I had trouble planning for the future since my future seemed so unknown. There was a chance this could kill me and erase my future entirely. There was a chance this lesion could paralyze me, which turned my future dark and hopeless. The worst part about it all? There was absolutely nothing I could do to alter its course or change it. Nada.

I think this state of helplessness made me obsessive-compulsive about the things I could control. Running made me feel good. It made me look darn good too! I always had a negative self-image, until I found running and saw it transform my body to what I had always wanted. Therefore, once I saw this, I obsessed over it. I never missed a day running. I was out there in the darkness, in the storm, and even on vacation when I should've been relaxing. It was an addiction. Some would say that is a pretty healthy addiction to have, but nothing is healthy when taken to extreme levels. I was not eating properly the way a person exercising so much should, so I got extremely skinny. My family will tell you it was too skinny, but I felt great in my own skin, for once.

Running was my escape from the constant thought of, "What if I had just had the surgery in Arizona or California?" I would put my headphones on, start running and just enjoy the smell of fresh air and the wind against my face. It was peaceful in a time of such chaos in my life.

I realized, in that moment, that thinking about all the "what ifs" did nothing for me, other than cause stress and depression. Like I have mentioned before, we must learn how to let go of "What if?" And learn to accept the "What is." I cannot change the past and see if a different outcome exists. Neither can you. There are actually lots of decisions we make in life that lead to different outcomes, like where you go to college, what major you study, and even what clothes you wear on any particular day. News flash, no matter what decision you make, there are always "What ifs" tied to it. Bummer, huh?

So why is all of this happening to me? I am a good person and try to be nice to those around me. Why me? This is so extremely unfair and should happen to a bad person, a murderer or something. I sat and cried many a time, thinking these before-mentioned words. Greg never seemed to understand or grasp my emotional pain and turmoil. At times, neither did my family. I would get so frustrated and angry with them, and that left me feeling more alone. Everyone would be so optimistic about things, when all I wanted was someone to just agree with me: This was unfair. But they couldn't understand what I was going through; no one could but me.

Even the people I would see out in public, and envy their non-bleeding brains and perfect lives, couldn't understand. They are most likely not living a perfect life, but to me as an outsider, it was all I could imagine.

Writing this now, I can see it from a different perspective. I am sure some of those people looked at me and thought I was living a perfect life and they were envious. You couldn't tell by just looking at me that my brain had a demon inside of it that just kept rupturing within its walls. With that being said, who was I to know, by looking at someone, that they had a perfect life? In reality, they may be suffering depression or just received a cancer diagnosis.

We have no idea the struggles other people face. That cashier at the grocery store who was rude to you? She may have just lost her husband in a horrible accident. The coworker who has a scowl on their face and ignores your attempts at friendly conversation? He may have just gotten diagnosed with Stage 4 cancer. We have no idea what other people are going through. How can we respond to a stranger's negative energy? Be respectful, be kind.

Optimistic thinking can be so hard to accomplish when one is faced with so much negativity. I was trying my best to live a full happy life, but my bleeding demon in my brain would not let me get too far without reminding me of its existence. From the brain bleeds, there were days I simply could not function. I called them Bad Brain Days, and they were just that. There were days I felt like I was having another bleed and would need to just take it easy and rest. These days were horrible, because no matter how hard I just wanted to forget my diagnosis, it would not let me do so. These were days I could not run or go to class; I had to lay in bed and sleep the Bad Brain Day away!

It wasn't fair. My college friends were maybe sleeping all day because they had a heavy drinking binge the night before, but here I was, living a healthy life and having to pay the price for something that wasn't my choosing.

What I did learn from these days was my adaptability. I saw that I was able to get through these days, and life does go on. Yes, in the midst of a Bad Brain Day I was very upset and wished they were not happening, but tomorrow was always there and my life could resume.

I read a quote one day that stated, "So far, you have survived 100% of your worst days. You're doing great." How powerful! We all have made it through our worst days, and if you ask me, that is a pretty darn good record to have.

Mom Here

Heather told me that this was a tough chapter for her to write. I understand that, it has the same feeling for me. I had seen her make the toughest decision, not only of her life, but one that few people in this world ever have to make. I know she made the right one, but how hard was it for her to decide that and then have this thing continue to bleed?

There were moments when I thought, if she had the surgery, at least we would know what we were dealing with. If she was paralyzed, we would figure it out. But at the time, brain surgery seemed to be a last choice.

Heather was functioning and doing relatively well, but I did see subtle physical changes that she may not have even noticed, such as holding her left arm behind her back or across her chest. My heart broke every time I saw this. I remember one day, walking out of the grocery store, and seeing a person walking with a cane; their left arm and left leg were in braces, obviously due to a brain injury. I immediately thought, is this going to be Heather, my beautiful 22-year-old daughter? Why? God, please let me know you got this.

I had a mantra at the time, "God is healing Heather!" I would constantly say this over and over to calm myself.

I was thankful that I have a strong faith in God and I had Him to lean on, especially when I got a call from Heather, who was away at college and having a "bad brain day." Was it another bleed? Should I drive there and bring her home?

They had given her a drug to help her sleep, and one night I got a call that she was hallucinating that the walls and floor were moving and smoke was coming under her bedroom door. She did not take that medicine again, and that was it for me to sleep that night.

I am sorry that you felt we did not recognize your struggle. I did and still do, but I believed that while I was praying for God to heal you, I knew that if not, He would give us the strength to get through it. There were times, and there still are, when I question why and am angry with God, but I know He can take it. He gave you the spirit and faith to shine in the darkness.

41

I did question what I believed to be God's silence. I never questioned His existence, but when you are being faithful and you don't think you are getting an answer, maybe you are not looking at it properly. My mantra, "God is healing Heather," was actually true, but I did not understand at the time.

Dad Here

I knew this situation was very serious and I felt very badly that this was happening to Heather. I did my best to support her in any ways she needed. I was determined to get her what she needed, when she needed it, with no consideration of time or money that needed to be expended.

I never questioned any of her decisions for Gamma Knife, or what she felt was best for her. She is a very smart person and these were all life-altering or life-ending decisions.

Optimistic is the way I'm wired. I see myself as a risk taker, let's get it fixed, tenacious to the nth degree, prayerful, confused about what to do next. How can I help Heather? I had never experienced anything like this before.

We'll get through this together, we are a strong, faithful family. God is going to reveal His plan. We need to be diligent about asking others for healing prayers. This is BIG, nasty, and out of our control.

When Heather would call from school, I would hold my breath, wondering, how is she doing? Good "brain day?" or "bad brain day?"

I was always thinking, how is she going to manage the demands of her college curriculum with her unpredictable condition? If she is having a bad day, that will affect Lynn and me. If it's a "good brain day," we were very thankful, at least for a short period.

The unknown is very stressful. I wished I could have taken this from her; that would allow her to enjoy her life, uninhabited by this monster in her head.

The Nightmare

Trying my best to accomplish just living my best life had its moments. There were days I couldn't take the struggle of having an inoperable brain tumor that could rupture at any given moment. There were days when the fear was too much to bear. I remember one particular day when I was in my college apartment, sobbing uncontrollably on the bathroom floor. The fear and uncertainty of my future were suffocating me and I started to draft my own suicide note. It was a note to my family and Greg, explaining that I decided to take my fate into my own hands, but I loved them and would always be with them.

As I was drafting this, my tears were soaking the page and I suddenly felt a moment of clarity that saved my life. Although my future was drastically unknown, what if it all turns out alright? Isn't every aspect in life unknown? There is no certainty that it will turn out badly. There is still a chance thing may turn out okay. I tore the darkest words I ever wrote into shreds and wiped my face.

How did I refocus my perspective? I put my eyes on God, the One who was in control of everything and already knew the outcome of my situation. There was something oddly comforting about the fact He was already in my future and knew exactly what was going to happen to me. I wish He would've shared this information with me, but at least I knew He was already there. However, I certainly couldn't have predicted what was coming next.

Desperate for another opinion on my situation after the fourth brain hemorrhage in only 10 months, we met a local neurosurgeon, Dr. Friedlander, Chief of Neurosurgery at UPMC, one of the best hospitals in the world. He gave me the same prognosis as all the other neurosurgeons I'd met before: Watch and wait. Despite him not giving me the magical solution, I had hoped for, my gut told me there was something special about him. He was unlike any neurosurgeon I'd met yet. He was personable, kind, and empathetic. I felt good about my decision to follow him with my treatment and use UPMC hospital for my care.

One fall day, my parents were at my college with me and we were meeting with my professors to ask for additional time on exams. My messy brain sometimes had trouble focusing, so this would help me do my best on exams. Hopefully, straight A's for Mom! We were walking all around campus, and after a while I noticed I was subconsciously holding my left arm across my chest while walking. I thought that was a strange thing to do, but it was the most comfortable position for whatever reason. It caused me to focus on how the rest of my body was feeling. How long had I been walking around like this? What else seemed off? Well, my left leg felt slightly weaker, and I did feel a little dizzy. We finished our day at my favorite restaurant for lunch, where I voiced my strange symptoms to my parents and Greg.

I also started to get a really bad headache, much like the one I had from the very first brain hemorrhage. We all decided, after so many false alarms, I should try and take a nap first, then see if I felt any better.

I did just that, in the hopes that one fantastic nap would make me feel normal and feel like I had nothing to worry about. You guessed it; I was wrong. I woke up from my nap not feeling normal and still concerned.

We drove the hour to the hospital back home, where everyone knew me by now; I was a regular. They ran some tests and I was all ready for the doctor to say I'd had another bleed. That was what I had come to expect. Bad news was my life. The doctor surprised me with the news there was no new blood in my brain, but the lesion was bigger, so they were going to admit me for observation. I was shocked. The symptoms I was feeling had me more than convinced I did have another bleed.

I spent the night in what was my now home away from home, the hospital. When I awoke the next morning, my whole life changed. I was paralyzed on the entire left side of my body. I still had two arms, but could only move one. I still had two legs, but could only move one. *This isn't good,* I had to admit to myself. To say I felt panic and fear is an understatement. Obviously, the medical team immediately did brain scans to see what was happening in my brain. News flash. That bloody demon had ruptured again! But this was its biggest performance to date: A massive hemorrhage in my brain that paralyzed my left side and miraculously did not kill me.

The doctor from the neurosurgery team came into my room to speak to my mom and me. He indicated they would be moving me to the Intensive Care Unit (ICU) and would be discussing my options, but most likely I would be having brain surgery to remove this uncontrollable lesion.

I had a headache beyond any headache you could ever imagine. Luckily, I was in a hospital that had many good drugs to help overcome the pain. So bear with me, the next few parts are a bit fuzzy for me. Whether it was the immense amount of blood in my brain or the strong drugs, who knows! My neurosurgeon, whom I had only seen a handful of times before, came into my ICU room to discuss my options. Well, there was really only one option at this point, I was going to be having brain surgery. Since the left side of my body was paralyzed now, and my lesion was bleeding uncontrollably and may kill me, there was no option but to remove it in its entirety.

Not to forget, brain surgery is no easy procedure! Especially in my case, the most important part of the brain could potentially be damaged during that operation, leaving me far worse off than I was half paralyzed. My neurosurgeon did what I like to call, "Reading my last rights," also known as telling me and my family the risks of such a surgery. I could be permanently paralyzed; have a different personality; be unable to talk; or could be in a coma. Or, there was the risk of me dying on the table.

Can I be honest here? Hearing all the risks and complications wasn't as scary as it might seem. At this point, I just wanted this demon thing out of my brain. It was almost as if I knew this was coming and it was expected. I thought that maybe, because that last hemorrhage has now paralyzed my body and taken away my last flicker of hope, I could no longer sit and wonder about all the unknowns. This was real, and there was no looking back.

45

I had a few days before my surgery. They wanted to run some experimental tests to make sure they had clearly defined the right path to go while inside my brain. UPMC actually had this special brain mapping technology and was the only hospital in the world to have it, so they were using it on my brain to determine the best way to extract the lesion. I couldn't complain; I didn't want them just poking around in there! I was reassured by the fact I was in one of the best hospitals in the world, UPMC, and one of the best neurosurgeons, Dr. Friedlander, would be performing my surgery. Over the next few days, while waiting for my procedure, the doctors were in and out of my room going over what to expect before, during, and after surgery.

One hospital staff member really sticks out to me. Every single morning at the crack of dawn, he would swing open my door, slam on all the lights and scream, "Heather!!!" It would startle me out of a dead sleep and I would say, "Yeah?" Then he would just leave! My mom and I laughed when we found out they charged my insurance hundreds of dollars for that morning wake-up call. Our health care system is surely confusing.

Obviously, there are a lot of risks associated with brain surgery. What was I most scared of? The part where I was most likely going to wake up from surgery with a breathing tube down my throat. This terrified me. Thinking I could wake up groggy, choking on something, and not able to communicate, nor understand what was going on. A very close family friend, Pastor Scott, the pastor of our church, came to visit me in the hospital and we prayed that I would not have to experience the terror of waking up with a breathing tube down my throat.

Then the day came, the day of my brain surgery. I said my, "See you later," to my family and Greg and they wheeled me off to the operating room. It was ridiculously early in the morning and they didn't allow me to wear contact lenses or glasses, without which I am blind, so I could not see where we were going exactly. We were in a room and I could hear some nurses and another patient in there with me. They were prepping us for surgery. All of a sudden, I heard a male voice say, "Hey, I hear you have a bun in the oven!" For those of you who may not understand, that is code for pregnant! When I heard this, my mouth dropped and my heart skipped a beat. *Pregnant? Greg and my family will surely be surprised to hear this!* Fortunately, I realized the male nurse was talking to another nurse, not me. *Phew!*

Back to business, brain surgery. They wheeled me into the operating room and my non-corrected eyesight could make out bright lights and fuzzy blobs of what I suspected were people. Then the familiar voice of my neurosurgeon Dr. Friedlander told me they were ready to get started and he would see me when it is all over. This was it. Was I scared I wouldn't wake up and this was the last moment of my life? Honestly, no.

Is that weird? I wasn't afraid of dying? I mean, sure it crossed my mind, and I certainly didn't want it to happen, but being a Christian makes death much less scary. I knew then, as I always have, that I will have eternal life, be reunited with family members who have passed before me, and live in absolute paradise. Doesn't sound too shabby does it? In addition, I just wanted to get this little demon out of me. It was impacting my life, and most recently, had paralyzed half my body, so it was due time to evict the tiny monster!

I also had the immense reassurance that I was in the best place in the world to undergo a procedure of this magnitude. This hospital was one of the absolute best in the world. They had brain mapping technology that could look at the actual fibers of my brain to determine the safest route for the neurosurgeon to take. How cool! I was truly in the right place at the right time. Not to forget, I knew one of the best neurosurgeons would be the one cutting into my brain. Dr. Friedlander was the best and had the best technology. I knew I was in good hands. It was all still scary, but slightly comforting, as comforting as brain surgery could be, I guess.

We never know what our reaction to a situation will be until we are in it. For example, had you told me, years before, that I would be having brain surgery after suffering a stroke at 23 years of age, I would have told you that you were crazy. Well, first I would have slapped you, then told you that you were crazy, and then I would cry. I would have thought, *there is no possible way that could happen to me, and if it did, there is no possible way I could handle that situation.* My first and foremost fear would have been death. But when it actually happened, that was not my main concern. We cannot think to ourselves, *Well, if this event happens to me, I will feel X way.* I hate to say it, but we can't predict what life situations will happen to us, nor can we predict what our reactions or feelings will be when they occur. Maybe it's best we don't know these things before they happen.

Then, in what seemed like a split second, I was slowly waking up from surgery. Guess what? I was waking up with no breathing tube! According to Dr. Friedlander, this was unheard of after the operation I had, but my prayers had been answered. Greg and my family were surrounding my bedside and as I was opening my eyes, Greg whispered in my ear, "You've never looked more beautiful to me than you do right now." I thought, *how incredibly sweet that was considering I knew half my head was shaved, I had tubes coming out of my skull, and I'm sure I had a pretty gnarly incision on my head. But thanks Greg, that was very romantic and sweet of you to say.* My sister Lauren was crying at the foot of my bed. I honestly wouldn't have expected anything else from her; she's a very emotional soul. I saw her tear-stained face and immediately tried to lighten the mood by saying, "Oh, stop crying! I'll be dancing at your wedding!!" This was apropos, since she was going to be getting married just six months from then.

Mom Here

Little did I realize, as we were driving to the emergency room yet again, that I was going to walk through the doors of that hospital and not walk out for three weeks. As the ER doctor informed us that this thing had now bled within itself and they wanted to admit her I once again, I was surprised and confused. When we arrived to Heather's room, there was a young woman in the bed next to her who was having a very difficult time. She had an inoperable brain tumor that was malignant. Her family was around her and I so remember her brother as he prayed with me and sent me a picture of Jesus standing next to the doctors in the operating room guiding their hands. Little did I know then what a comfort that would give me and many others in the future.

I decided to stay at the hospital that night. So began my journey of locating places to sleep. Since Heather had a roommate, I was not permitted to stay in her room, even though I had already become quite an expert at sleeping in chairs during all of her hospital stays. Not that there was a lot a sleeping, as anyone who has been in the hospital knows.

My heart broke often for my daughter. Many times, I randomly broke down in tears as I thought of what her life had become, her constant threat of a brain bleed, and no medical options available to her. Such a rare disease and such a dangerous location in her brain! As any parent would say, I wished it was me and not her. She had already gone through so much with the bullying and bipolar train.

They often say God gives you only what you can handle. I have to disagree. I believe He may give you more, so you reach out to Him. I used to say my prayers while sitting in a chair. I was now praying prone, face down on the floor, begging for just enough strength to get through the day.

The next morning, about 5:30 a.m., I went downstairs to get a cup of coffee for myself and Heather. When I got to her room, she asked if I would help her get to the bathroom. As we did, she realized the left side of her body was not moving. So, fast forward to another CT scan, neurosurgeon conference, and resident coming in to say she had a massive bleed that shifted the midline of her brain 4mm and they feared it was blocking the spinal fluid from draining from her brain. They were taking her to the NeuroICU. They were 45% sure she would need a drain placed in her brain, and 85% sure she would need brain surgery. Talk about your world spinning. *How did we get here? How was this possible?*

I stepped out in the hall to call her dad and saw my eldest daughter coming down the hall. I broke down in tears. Lauren consoled me and was by my side the rest of the day. Luckily, I was able to pull myself together. My MO is to be strong in a crisis and fall apart later. I needed to continue to be there for Heather and my family

Not sure if you remember, but we had asked our church and friends to pray to stop this thing from bleeding, and my mantra was, "God is healing Heather." The bleeding continued and I was questioning God. Well, sure enough, He had a plan. Because of the continued bleeds and this last massive one, the angioma had been pushed to a place the neurosurgeon could reach it. God knew better all the time. Even when we question if He has heard our prayers, He knows what we do not know.

Heather is a little fuzzy on some of the details, as she was getting some very powerful pain killers. I, on the other hand, got squat! They really should have a program to allow the mom to get something, even if it's just a glass of wine.

As we waited for the specialized MRI and further tests, as can be expected in an ICU, several of the folks admitted there did not survive. It was heartbreaking to see these families hear the news and leave. You are momentarily joined at one of the worst times of your life. You hear stories of their loved ones and gain insight into others' lives. You cry together and pray together. I remember praying with a woman in the chapel, and the next morning as I was straddled between two chairs trying to sleep, she was covering me with a blanket. I was so deeply touched. The nights after I had to leave Heather's room to find a place to lay my head were the worst. I was usually huddled in a corner of a waiting room, with nothing else to do but think. That can make for a very long, lonely night. Your mind goes places you never thought you would ever go. When I left the ICU, I always checked with the nurse to make sure they had my cell number. I let them know I would be down the hall if something changed. I did not want Heather to be alone if things went from bad to worse. I asked God to help her and guide the surgeons to come up with the best possible solution. If Heather were to die, would that at least give her some relief? I could not wrap my head around that outcome, but I did not want her to suffer.

Our dear friends of 30 years would bring a meal to the hospital and sit with us. On the nights my husband went home, he would stop at their house and they would bring out his "take-out" meal.

I could not fathom driving home and being 20 minutes away. What would I do if something happened? I had to be by her side at every moment. I even got a tip of a secret shower from a nurse who had not been able to leave because of a snowstorm. That turned out to be a great help. My husband would bring me a change of clothes and I would sneak away for a few moments to clean up. Ultimately, a large hospital has all of the essentials of life. I pondered if I was homeless, needing a place to sleep, I could probably have wandered around a hospital for at least a week before staff would get suspicious.

The big day was here. As we said goodbye to Heather, her last

50

words to us as she was being wheeled down the hall were, "What am I going to do about my finals?"

Really? That is what you are worried about? Those must be good drugs you are getting. The surgery took nine hours. I remember watching the screen that lets you know where they are and when it said "Surgery Started," I thought I was going to pass out. They were now opening my daughter's brain. We had family and friends there, waiting and praying with us. At one point my dad came over and slipped his hand in mine and just sat quietly with me. As the waiting room was emptying out, and I saw we were the last family there, I heard the phone ring at the receptionist's desk. She called our name and I went over and picked up the phone and heard Dr. Friedlander's voice saying all was completed, no breathing tube, and she was in recovery. Praise the Lord, my daughter had survived. The bonus was when she said to her sister, "Oh, stop, I'll be dancing at your wedding!". I knew then that our Heather was still there.

God's answers are not always the ones we expect. We may be praying for one thing and get frustrated when our prayers are not answered, but God's plans are there for a reason. Maybe they will become clear as ours did, but maybe not.

Dad Here

As a dad, all I wanted to do was take care of, and love my family. What Heather was going through was not due to something she did or didn't do. This was a very rare medical condition. All-of-a-sudden, it decided to afflict my daughter and disrupt our entire family life.

When Heather asked us if we could come to school and support her by visiting her professors to request special accommodations for taking her final exams, after she had persevered through months of suffering and overcoming her medical condition all semester, I thought, *Sure. These professors will understand and will give her credit for hanging in and working hard to maintain her grades once they know what she has been dealing with.*

Well, some were cordial and accommodating, while some were just full of their self-importance and challenging. We presented our requests to the professors as a loving and concerned family, not realizing that in a couple of hours all this was going to dramatically change, and we would be headed to the hospital instead of home.

The next day I was at work and got the call that Heather was going to be moved to the Intensive Care Unit and that I should come immediately. Not what I wanted to hear nor what I had been praying for. I took a few steps leaving my office, and fell to my knees, crying. *Why was this happening to Heather?*

In the ICU, when Dr. Friedlander spoke to Heather, all I can remember hearing is, "We need to get this thing out or it will kill you." *What would we do? How very different our lives would be. This is my* "little Dinky," *my little buddy. God is not going to take her away yet.* I thought, *well that certainly answers my question concerning next steps.*

As they are wheeling Heather down the hall to surgery, she asked us, "What am I going to do about finals?" First, I thought she was nuts and why was she worried about school? Then I thought, wow, this gives me an opportunity to help her while she's in the operating room. I will reach out to all her professors and work to get them to waive her final exams and just base her final grade on the level of work she had already done. She will not be back to school this semester, and at this point, I wasn't sure if she would ever return to school.

My biggest fear was the thought of losing her. The next thought was a possible cognitive deficit that would affect her for the rest of her life. As far as I was concerned, I was 100% committed to helping her, no matter what that meant to me personally, financially or professionally. Regarding her professors, some responded favorably and all but one agreed to use her current grade standing in their class. The one who would not agree initially was finally persuaded on Christmas Eve; he sent us his approval for dropping her one letter grade for missing the final. She still passed the class without having to repeat it.

The night of her brain surgery, there was a time in the ICU when I was alone with Heather. She had so many tubes and devices hooked up to her. I had no idea what the purpose was for any of them, but felt she was in a very good place to be taken care of. In deep prayer, I sat next to her bed asking God to put His healing hands on her and allow her to recover from this horrific challenge. God showed me a vision as clear as could be. First, He showed me her walking down the aisle at her sister's wedding. Then He showed me walking her down the aisle at her own wedding. Then He showed her back in a hospital bed. My initial reaction to that last part was of great concern that something bad may have happened to her, but as I looked closer, I realized she was pregnant and this was a good thing. Then, as clearly as if the voice was in the room, God told me, "Tell Heather to have a wonderful life".

In front of me was a tray with some napkins on it. So I grabbed one and wrote the note from God to Heather, "Go have a wonderful life." I had that experience captured in a note and framed the napkin with the message from God. She has that hanging in her home as a daily reminder that God has big plans for Heather, and she is going to have a wonderful life.

The Grit

I can still remember the disappointment when I woke up from surgery and realized the left side of my body was still paralyzed. Not one doctor told me that the brain surgery would restore my mobility, but deep down, I had hoped a miracle would occur. What I didn't realize was, the miracle was that I was alive, not cognitively affected, and that bleeding demon was finally out of my head! This was just the first page of the new chapter of my life. I had no idea what lay ahead of me.

I spent a few weeks at the hospital where I had my brain surgery. There was one night that brought some comical relief. We were in my room, when all of a sudden, a code was called and the doors automatically locked. It was not a medical emergency, but rather one of the patients was running down the hall naked with his pee bag in hand. Never a dull moment on the Neuro floor of the hospital! Or there was the time my mom had to yell at a nurse because my Intracranial Pressure sensor was going off with alarms. Obviously, this sparked Momma Bear!

Speaking of bears, I saw some while in the hospital. Yes, you read that correctly. I was napping and saw these three bears sitting outside my hospital room at a picnic table. When I awoke, still groggy from the nap and the pain medication, my mom told me that my grandparents were coming to visit me. I immediately sparked up and said, "Tell them to watch out for the bears! Especially the brown ones, they are really mean!" Oh boy. The only explanation I can think of for this was the mixture of the strong drugs they were giving me and the teddy bear that Greg's friend gave me that sat in my room. This freaked out my mom enough that she told Dr. Friedlander not to give me more of the hard stuff. When she explained to him why, he replied in the best way possible, "I've seen those bears." *Thanks for the backup, Doc!*

I do not remember much from my time immediately after surgery, but I do remember the start of my recovery; that was the day I was transferred to an in-patient rehab facility. This place was where my journey officially began. I would undergo physical and occupational therapy day-in-and-day-out to try to regain as much function as possible. When you just had a massive stroke and major brain surgery, this is no easy feat!

Once again, I found myself in the right place at the right time. This was another hospital of UPMC and it was the best of the best. At UPMC Mercy, I was fortunate enough to be assigned a Dr. Galang, who would oversee my rehab treatment. He was funny, and I could tell he was very passionate about helping people recover. What a blessing he was to me when I felt almost helpless; he brought such a light and enthusiasm into my life!

What does it feel like to have half your body paralyzed? Well, it is like looking at an inanimate object and willing it to move with your brain powers. Picture a rock in your lap, and you are staring at it long and hard, trying to move it, but no matter how hard you try, it just stays in the same place. Imagine that, but with your own body! Raise your hand above your head. See how easy that was? You barely have to think about it. Now try and wiggle your ears. Takes more brain power to wiggle your ears, right? If you're one of those people who can wiggle their ears, then cool, but if you are sitting there trying so hard to wiggle them, but they aren't budging, welcome to my world.

Except this is the feeing I get trying to move the left side of my body. I know it's there and I can picture it moving, but no matter how hard I try, nothing.

It was as if my brain had completely forgotten its existence. I can remember what it felt like to move it, to walk, but now it is as if my left arm and leg have turned to stone, just a heavy weight, with no life. Oh, how I took for granted the ability to move my body!

This was hard to accept as my new reality, but I had no other choice. It wasn't like I could pretend it wasn't real, close my eyes, and magically be normal again. Believe me, I tried! I chose to face this battle head-on. I suppose I could have given up and decided to just live in this new reality as it was given to me. No way, Jose! I was able to accept this as my reality *right now,* but I was not willing to accept this as my new reality *forever!* I would not be in a wheelchair the rest of my life. Well, I might not have much choice in that matter, but I am going to do everything in my power to make sure I can walk!

I remember when I arrived at the new hospital for my rehab and they said they were taking me to my room on the Stroke Unit. I thought that was such a shocking thing, a 23-year-old is going to the Stroke Unit. I don't think that was a sentence I ever imagined hearing in my life, especially at this young age.

When you get hit with an unforeseen circumstance, and feel hopeless and powerless, just find that power in your choice of how to face it. You have power and hope, but they reside within your heart. Life is cruel and unfair; I think we can all agree with that statement. It hits all of us differently, but one thing guaranteed is, it will hit. Actually, our entire existence is just a sequence of things happening to us, good and bad.

We all are just fighting our way through life and making it to our eternal glory that God has promised. None of us will make it out of this life alive, but we all will make it out. So, what happens when life hits you hard? You may feel as though you have no options and your life is out of control, but that is not true. No matter your situation, you always have two options: Whether you throw up your hands and succumb to your situation as your new reality, or you decide to focus on what you can do to fight against your circumstances, it is up to YOU to decide.

I chose to do everything within my power to fight. How did I do that? I honestly am not sure I ever thought there was an option of not giving it my all. I did know that I didn't want to be in a wheelchair for the rest of my life, and there were things in life I wanted to accomplish. So, every day in inpatient rehab, I did hours of physical and occupational therapy and did both to the very best of my ability. Were there times I was too tired and frustrated and wanted to just give up? Absolutely! Actually, when I first started inpatient rehab, I was dealing with extreme nausea and moving too much caused me to vomit. My first few days in therapy, I gave it my all... including my breakfast!

Knowing what my life would be like if I did not give it my all, kept me motivated. Now, there was a chance I could never walk again, despite a huge effort of rehab and dedication. There was a chance all the hard work I was putting in would not pay off. But there was a chance that it would pay off, and I would walk again. I do not know about you, but I would rather try and fail, than not try and wonder what would have happened if I had.

Being paralyzed sucks. I remember there were nights I would wake up and desperately need to use the restroom. Before this journey, I simply would just get out bed and walk to the bathroom, do my thing, and walk back into bed. But those days were gone; things had changed. Now when needing to use the restroom in the middle of the night, I needed to call for a nurse to get me out of bed, wheel me to the restroom, help me on to the toilet, wait for me to finish, help me back into my wheelchair, wheel me back to my bed, and help me in it again. It was a complicated process. One night, I awoke from a dead sleep with the urge to go to the bathroom. I called the nurse and he said he would be in soon to take me to the facilities. I waited... and waited... but no nurse. I called him again and got the same, "I'll be there soon." I waited... and waited... but then it happened, the warm feeling that is both relieving and uncomfortable at the same time. I had wet the bed. I remember calling my mom and crying because I was a 23-year-old who just wet the bed. I feared she would say, "No more horses for you," and I was so humiliated that I, at this age, could do something so juvenile! Sure, there are 23-year-olds at college who do this on a semi-weekly basis, but that is from heavy drinking, not my situation. Not fair. Not fair at all.

Then there was another night I found myself in a similar predicament. It was Christmas Eve, to be exact, and I had rung for the nurse a few times but still continued waiting. I felt the urgency becoming stronger and I decided there was no way I was going to soil myself again. I eagerly tried to find a way out of this humiliating experience. I looked around the room and saw my wheelchair, only about three feet from my bed. I thought, *surely, I can just stand up out of bed and walk one step to my chair, then wheel myself into the bathroom and back. That doesn't seem too outrageous of a plan.* Well, I got up and went to take that step to my chair, but very quickly fell to the floor like a sack of potatoes. Of course, that was the exact moment the nurse ran into my room and saw what I had tried to do; she just started yelling at me for trying such a dangerous act. I was scheduled to go home for a few hours the next day and spend time with my family on Christmas, but the nurse warned me, since I fell, they may not allow me my few hours of freedom. At that point, I realized it may have been better to soil the bed and not remind myself how helpless and dependent I was in my current state.

They did allow me to go home for a little while on Christmas, and I honestly think that fall made me work that much harder on my recovery. I got sick in the car on the way home that Christmas Day. It was not what I had planned, but I was so excited to go home and see my family. Before we made it to the house, I begged my parents to make a stop at the barn so I could see my beloved horse, Darius. It was a very different experience at the barn, since I could not just walk in and see him, but my parents opened the car door and brought Darius to me so I could give him a smooch. As you know, riding was such a big part of my life and the goal of riding kept me motivated in my recovery.

The purpose of my inpatient rehabilitation was creating new brain pathways to my left side. The brain hemorrhage/ stroke damaged the pathways I had before, so now my brain had trouble accessing that side of my body. But when there's a will, there's a way, right? So, through determination, will, and repetitive movements, my brain created new pathways to the affected parts. It's amazing, but to do all this brain trailblazing took an enormous amount of energy. It was exhausting. And when you are living with a brain injury, brain exhaustion is the worst kind.

One day, when I was working on walking and I walked the furthest yet, down the hall to my bedroom, I climbed into bed in the middle of the afternoon and didn't wake up until the next morning. I remember asking my mom when dinner was, because I woke up starving; she informed me that I had slept through dinner but breakfast should be coming soon. In a nutshell, I slept for about 16 hours straight. I was getting a ton of sleep after my therapy sessions, but I heard that sleep was when the brain repaired itself, so sleep away, Heather!

Sometimes I think we don't listen to our bodies enough. We run around, pushing ourselves constantly, and our bodies try to tell us we need rest, but we choose to ignore them, because the rest will just get in the way of our plans.

First, we all need to find that one thing that motivates us. It usually is a defining moment in your life, or rock bottom if you will, that give us that extra push. The defining moment in my recovery was falling, just trying to go to the bathroom. I realized, in that moment, how incapable I was of self-care. This was just not acceptable to me and motivated me to do everything I could to change it. Second, you need to learn how to rest when your body is in dire need of it. Yes, we need to work hard to reach our goals, but we also need to allow time for rest and healing. Much like the day I slept for 16 hours straight, my body was in need of some major rest.

Mom Here

Shortly after Heather returned to NeuroICU from surgery, Dr. Friedlander came in to do a post-op exam. I could see the disappointment on his face when she could not move her left leg. My heart broke once again. Heather spent the next several days heavily medicated and sleeping most of the time. We would sit quietly, watching "The Heather Show," as we called it. I do remember watching a Steelers game with the sound off and silently cheering when they made a touchdown.

Heather had more tubes and wires connected to her than I had ever seen. There were the typical heart, blood pressure, oxygen monitors, and IV's. She also had two tubes coming out of her 15" incision. One allowed blood to drain and the other monitored her inter-cranial pressure. The nurse explained that if the pressure went above a certain level, it meant she was hemorrhaging. Ok, so I certainly kept my eye on that one. The time came to move her to a step-down unit, which actually was nine floors above where we were. I always thought that was funny.

Because Heather was classified as a stroke patient, that was the floor we were sent to. The majority of that population was elderly, thankfully so. Shortly after our arrival, the cranial pressure alarms started going off. Yup, you guessed it, I was in the full Momma Bear mode. When the nurse came in, she said, "Well, we don't see many of these on this floor, but I'm sure it's OK." *What? My daughter has had five hemorrhages in 11 months, brain surgery, and I was told how critical this was and that is your answer!* I asked for an ICU nurse to come up and check it. He explained, after it was in place for a while, they became less effective, so he removed it. That would have been nice to know.

As Heather said, since we are talking about bears, that happened exactly how she said. Naturally, my reaction was acceptable, heavy drugs and hallucinations. Dr. Friedlander's reaction was classic, "I've seen those bears." He took the tension down several levels. He also knew the amount of pain Heather was in, and she needed that medication, right now.

I was now able to sleep in Heather's room, as she had no roommate. Little sleep occurred as they came in every two hours to do a neuro check. Then the day came when they were going to transfer her to an inpatient rehab facility. Once again, I called my former boss and asked him where he thought she should go. He suggested she go to the facility where he was working so he could keep tabs on her. He would not be her physiatrist, as he was on the spinal cord unit, but he could follow her. So off we went, on a cold, rainy December day. The ambulance staff wrapped her up carefully so all you could see were her eyes. The next chapter had begun.

It was also a huge change for me. I went home that night. I slept in my own bed. I was so very nervous leaving her, but I had no other choice. I left after she fell asleep and was at her bedside, with our traditional coffee, before she woke up.

That first day of therapy was a rough one for Heather. We had created a Facebook page, "Heather's Fight for Therapy," where I had been posting updates. That day I said, "Heather gave it her all in therapy today, even her breakfast." She often became nauseous with movement. Not a good combination for therapy. I remember sitting there that first day and watching a gentleman walk around with a cane and perform several different steps for the therapist, walk over rough surfaces, go up and down steps, and step over larger objects. It brought tears to my eyes; all I could think was whether Heather would ever be able to do that. As of then, she was like a rag doll when I transferred her from bed to wheelchair, to the toilet, into a shower chair, and back.

The praying continued.

After the phone call from Heather about the bed-wetting incident, I arrived at the facility and asked to speak to the charge nurse. I expressed my disappointment that a person who has been through what she has been through should not have to deal with that. They assured me they would look into it, and that it would not happen again.

A couple hours later, they came back to tell me that Heather had tested positive for MRSA. What? I had no idea what that meant, other than knowing people died from it. As I came to better understand, she was a carrier of MRSA. Most folks who have spent that much time in a hospital usually are. The benefit was, Heather got a private room which she later called "Her Cave." She liked it dark and cold.

The physiatrist I know would usually stop by in the mornings to check on her. He gave her a bracelet that said "Fortitude" on it. She certainly showed that.

One other day that is seared into my memory was the first day they had her stand up and try to walk. If you remember, I spent most of my professional career in a facility like this, watching folks try every day. However, this was my baby. For a brief second, I thought to myself, *I cannot watch this, it is too painful.* Then I heard a voice say, "Yes, you can, she needs you and I am here with you." Thank-you, Lord.

Heather is right in saying that bad stuff happens every day; we need to choose how we move forward. Ok, so rehab it is.

Christmas morning came and I was excited and a little nervous to bring Heather home for a few hours. I got to her room and her physiatrist, Dr. Galang, was there, examining her because of her fall. He was actually very sweet about it. While he made sure she would never try it again, he said, "No harm, no foul, you can go home." So off we went.

Pittsburgh is a city of bridges and when we were crossing the first one, I had to jump out because Heather had gotten sick, and I had to dump the bucket into the Monongahela.

We did have a wonderful day at home, but before we went there, Heather made us stop at the barn to see her horse. I brought him out

61

to the car and she gave him a big kiss on the nose.

We never know what life is going to ask of us. Our initial reaction may be, *I cannot handle that, there is no way.* Yes, there is a way. For me, my faith is what gave me the courage and strength to get through. I would be failing if I didn't encourage you to seek God, but if that is not in your present, there are many ways to get help and figure it out. My eldest daughter is a psychologist and helps folks figure it out every day.

Dad Here

Ok, now what? What can we expect? What can I do to help? What is Heather going to act like? Why the heck are we moving her to another hospital? Where are we going on Christmas day before we get her home for a few hours?

My biggest fear was losing Heather in surgery. My next biggest fear was how all of this was going to affect her cognitively and physically. This was totally new territory and I am the type of person who needs to assess the situation, create a plan, and execute it, making adjustments as we go, to work as a team for a common goal. Yet I watched my baby go from an athlete to a totally dependent person on very heavy pain medicines, and remnants of her brain surgery, from her shaved head to her million stitches holding her skull together.

Now you want to move her to another hospital. Her surgeon is here and I have finally figured out how to get around here, and you want me to go somewhere else.

As it turns out, the hospital where she is being moved had the word "Mercy" in its name; that may be defined as, "a fortunate thing; kind or compassionate treatment; relief of suffering; blessing." This hospital had nuns working there, and an active church on the first floor, which we attended as a family (Heather in a wheel chair) on Christmas Eve...not to mention all the time I spent on my knees in prayer in that church.

Heather has always been competitive, but this was a whole new fight ahead of her. I was so proud to see her deep determination to recover, not to let this hold her back, she was going to win.

When I watched her in physical and occupational therapy, I always wanted to answer the question or physically help her move. There were times when I would think, if she quits and says, "I can't do this anymore." I will understand. But I knew that only she could do this, and that she would.

I needed to be there to encourage, to point out the slightest of improvements and accomplishments as I saw them. To pray quietly, yet intently, for every step and movement, for God to put His healing hands on her and give her the strength she needed to persevere.

As we were driving her home on Christmas day, I was told we needed to make a stop on the way. *Are you kidding me? You want to go and see the horse? I am so afraid of anything bad happening while we are out and in my care. You want to go to a barn which is a dirty environment? How are we going to get her into the barn? What does she think she is going to do once we get to the stable, ride the horse, groom the horse, feed the horse?*

The New Normal

While in the inpatient rehab facility, I had a very structured schedule of therapy each and every day. They come to your room and get you, whether you want to or not. As my mom mentioned, I was having a lot of trouble with motion sickness. Any movement, even just moving my head, would cause me to throw up. *Kind of embarrassing when you are in a room full of strangers! But the show must go on.* I would work through the throwing up in an effort to regain as much mobility as possible. My mind was set on one goal: I was not going to let anything get in the way of achieving it.

I spent the holidays in the rehab facility. Christmas was when I got to go home with my family for a few hours. In typical Heather fashion, I had to make things difficult for my poor parents and make them stop so I could see my horse. Since I couldn't walk into the barn, they brought him out to the car so I could give him a quick pet and a smooch.

On New Year's Eve, Greg came to the rehab to be with me. He wheeled me down to the cafeteria, then wheeled me up to the top floor to watch the fireworks over the city. How romantic! It was another hard reality for me, spending New Year's in a hospital with no champagne toast at midnight. At least I didn't have to worry about the hangover the next morning.

Time dragged on while I was in the rehab facility. All I wanted was to go home and be with my family. Then the day came when my wish came true, they were sending me home. This dream came true with mixed emotions. Sure, I was going home, going to sleep in my own bed, and not have to worry about wetting the bed anymore, but I was leaving the only place I knew in my new reality. I was leaving a safe place, filled with wonderful doctors and nurses, and a structured therapy regimen. I was leaving my security. *I have not been in the outside world in this new body of mine.*

In the hospital, they tried to prepare me as best they could for potential difficulties I would face daily in my new body, such as how to get dressed with only one arm, how to sit down and stand up without losing my balance, and how to safely bathe myself in my condition. *Oh, how my life has changed. Most girls my age were learning how to contour their makeup or apply different styles of eyeliner. Not me! I'm learning how to sit in a chair without breaking my neck!* Anyway, the hospital staff did so much to prepare me for my big homecoming, but I was filled with such anxiety and fear when the day came closer.

My anxiety was overwhelming at times. Here in the hospital, I had nurses on whom I could be completely dependent, but at home I would be completely dependent on my parents. *Yes, I am sure my parents will come quickly at night when I need to go to the bathroom, but they were my parents; they don't deserve to have to care for me like this. The nurses at the hospital were paid to take care of me, my parents have raised me and shouldn't have this responsibility.*

I felt like such a burden, like maybe it would have been better if I had died in surgery. Of course, they would be sad, but I wouldn't be a constant hindrance to their normal lives. These are pretty dark thoughts, right? I couldn't help but feel them, and the fear associated with my new disability in the real world. *How am I going to navigate the stairs at my house? Or am I just going to live in the basement? How will I endure being such a burden on my family?*

When we feel those dark thoughts, we need to accept them as our thoughts, but that's it. They are just thoughts, and not necessarily truths. Most of our thoughts are irrational. I'm not saying to ignore them and stuff them down. Acknowledge them as your feelings, but also be aware they are irrational. I knew my parents loved me more than words could explain, and want to be there for me and take care of me. They knew I would not give up this fight, and they want to be there every step of the way.

The big day finally came. I got to go home! It was not the smoothest transition, since I was still struggling with extreme motion sickness and threw up multiple times on the car ride home. I remember getting angry with my mom, telling her to avoid bumps in the road, but that was an impossible thing to ask of her. *Sorry, Mom.* We finally made it home after the horrific car ride, and I was immediately faced with the gut-wrenching reality of my situation. My parents had to bring me into my house via the front door. I know that doesn't sound like such a terrible thing, but for some reason it was a trigger for me. My entire life, up until this moment, I had entered my home through the garage. You park the car in the garage, go in through the basement door, climb the stairs, and you're in! But since I still could not conquer stairs safely, they wheeled me down the sidewalk to the front door. I kept a brave face for my parents, but on the inside, I was flooded with painful emotion.

Was this going to be the rest of my life? Why did God let this happen to me? How will Greg deal with his future wife being so useless? As these emotions of giving up came over me, I felt this push in my heart to just close my eyes and pray. I prayed to God to give me the strength to fight this, to just keep going. I made sure He knew my anger towards my situation, of which He already knew. Then I was given a memory that gave me the guidance I was seeking. The memory was of my mom, during my depression, telling me that there are days you just don't have the motivation to go on, but all you have to do is make your bed. In a nutshell, she was saying to just do what you can that day.

The takeaway here is, you may have these giant plans and goals to achieve, but you're not going to accomplish all of them in one day. All you can do is focus on today, and do as much or as little as you want. Psychologists say the best way to achieve a big goal is to set small goals along the way that are easier to attain and will help keep you motivated. All you have to do today is make your bed. For me, this was immensely comforting and changed my perspective on my recovery. I was looking at the big picture too much, focusing on the entire negative. But I changed my perspective and decided I was just going to do what I could each day and that's it. My big goal was to walk again without any walking aides, but that was going to take time. *If I put in the work, a little each day, then I will achieve my goal! Well, hopefully.*

That first night at home was nice. My mom got to experience the life of a hospital nurse. I would call her when I needed to use the restroom and she would come right away. No more wetting the bed for me! I had the equipment I had to sleep with on my person, so we would call it "strapping Heather in." It was a nightly ritual. Greg stayed at my parents' house in the spare bedroom for a while. It was nice having him close by, but difficult to feel connected to my fiancé with my dad in the next room. I did just what I had set my mind to. Every day, I did my therapy and did as much or as little as I felt like.

I remember at this point I was starting to walk with a cane. I would do laps around the first floor, with my mom walking beside me, I tried to do a set number of laps before calling it a day.

Leaving the hospital, I was scared to lose the scheduled therapy every day, because I knew at home it would be so easy to just skip out on my therapy. But then came my mom. She kept me on schedule, and even thought of creative new exercises to try. She is amazing! People often ask me how I did it. How did I stick to doing my exercises every day and to not give up? Honestly when you are that disabled, that dependent on other people, and there is a chance you have the power to change that; you just do everything you can.

I honestly just did it. Plus, my parents were so immensely supportive. If I gave up, I wouldn't just be letting myself down. I wanted to walk down the aisle at my wedding.

The hardest part about being home was the bathing. I could not safely stand up in the shower, so I had a shower chair I sat on, but my mom had to help with every step of the process. I know she had seen me naked as a kid, but I was an adult now. Awkward. She did her best to make it comfortable, but there was no avoiding it. She helped shave my legs and dry me off. To me, bathing was meant to be a private experience, but for me those days were gone. As an adult, this was difficult to swallow. I guess she finally saw that tattoo I never told her about, but on a more serious note, I couldn't help but feel like I had regressed in my life. It was as if I was no longer an adult, but had transported back to being a baby.

I felt trapped in my own body. My mind was still an adult's, but my body was an infant's, incapable of self-care. Was this going to my new life?

I started going to an out-patient rehab facility a few days a week. The ironic part was, this was a facility where my mom used to work years before, when I was just a twinkle in her eye. I am sure it was hard for her to be on the other side of services offered.

Mom Here

As the days continued through in-patient rehab Heather's determination never wavered. She worked hard every day and made steady improvements. The therapists were wonderful and got to experience some of Heather's humor. When she would get frustrated, she would make a joke about it. During one occupational therapy session, they had her left arm strapped to an arm support connected to a computer screen. There were various video games that she needed to move her left arm to complete. One of them was steering a car with a chicken in it and keeping them on the road. May I say things ended badly for the chicken. Heather's response was, "Chickens shouldn't be driving anyway." Point well taken.

While her left arm and hand were slow to recover, her left leg was making progress. Remember that first day in therapy, when I wondered if Heather would ever be able to do what that man with the cane was doing? Well, she was. She was walking with a cane for short distances, and they had her going up and down a few steps. She still needed the wheelchair, as she tired easily.

When the news came to bring her home, we were so very excited. I put my rehabilitation worker hat on and looked around the house to see how we could make it as comfortable as possible. We moved her bed closer to the wall so she would have more room for the wheelchair; we acquired and assembled a shower chair and a shampoo and conditioner dispenser in the wall, so she would be able to use her right hand to get that. We set up a television in her room and got her a new mattress since she would be spending more time there. I moved her toothbrush and make-up to the first-floor powder room so she could freshen up without having to climb the stairs. We planned one trip down in the morning and one trip up in the evening. OK, I was ready.

We brought Heather home and that day she immediately went to bed; the car ride wore her out. I sat down at the kitchen table with her array of medications and made a chart. She was on medications for pain, seizure prevention, antibiotics, blood thinners, nausea, and constipation due to the pain killers. I didn't want to give her the wrong amount or at the wrong time. I remember walking into the pharmacy one day and the clerk said, "Hello, Lynn, how are you?" I thought to myself, *I don't know that this is a good thing I am on a first name basis at the pharmacy.*

At night I put our old baby monitor in her room so I could hear her when she needed to go to the bathroom. The brain injury had left her with urgency. When she would call, I would run in, get her into her wheelchair, fly to the bathroom, transfer her, and wait outside for her to call. I have to say the nightly rendezvous did remind me of when she was an infant and needed a bottle at night.

I know the shower situation was going to be tough on her. She was always a very private person about her body. I tried as much as I could to give her as much independence and privacy as possible. Come to think of it, maybe her modesty about her body was that she didn't want me to find the tattoos. Hmm.

Beside the emotional toll this had taken on all of us, there was also a financial one. We did have good health insurance, thank God, but the overall bill for Heather's stay in the hospital, her brain surgery, and in-patient rehabilitation, was over half-million dollars. We had spent close to $24,000 out of pocket, not including my loss of work time, gas, and meals. We were in no way complaining or sorry; we had our Heather. That was all that mattered. A new challenge had arisen.

While the health insurance covered most catastrophic costs, outpatient therapy was limited to 22 visits a year. Heather needed to go three days a week and she was going to need way more than that. The blessing of working in the rehabilitation field in my prior life was, I did know a few avenues to go down to make that happen. I started filling out applications for Social Security Disability, but I knew there was a waiting period and it was going to be an uphill battle to get approved.

In our state, there is a great organization called The Office of Vocational Rehabilitation. They will often assist with therapy costs with the goal of getting the individual back to work and contributing to society. Thankfully, Heather was approved, so when our insurance ran out, they took over.

While this was a difficult time for us all, we pulled together as a family to get things done. Heather did her part by working harder than I ever expected. Her sister surprised her by arranging for someone to come to the house and give her a new hairstyle to cover the huge scar on her skull. Her fiancé stuck by her and would make her some special dinners. Her dad arranged for an amazing fundraiser at a top shelf restaurant, with entertainment, wine, and a silent auction to help pay for her therapy. One fond memory I have of that time is, in the evening after we got Heather into bed and "strapped in," one of us would crawl into bed beside her and the other would sit in her wheelchair; it had a special arm rest for her left arm that you could set a drink on, and we would talk, watch tv, or just snuggle. It showed how much we truly loved one another

Life is challenging. I am blessed to have a supportive family, friends, and God. If one of those is lacking in your life, there are outside organizations that can offer support. Do not be afraid to ask and explore them; that is what they are there for.

Dad Here

What always impressed me was Heather's determination. She was not going to let this beat her. How could I help?

As I reflect on bringing her home, I was glad that I wouldn't need to go to the hospital each day to visit. I was concerned about being able to handle her physical needs.

I often thought this would be the way it was, with arranging and possibly remodeling our home so Heather could basically live on the first floor in a wheelchair. *What modifications should we make to accommodate her new needs? Should we sell the house and move into something better suited for her limitations?*

I love Heather and wanted to do whatever was best for her. We had been so very blessed to travel and participate in exciting activities and sports, such as snow skiing and horseback riding. *If that is all over now, I am accepting of my new normal, staying home and just enjoying the fact that she is alive and home.*

For whatever reason, I felt compelled to take pictures of Heather from ICU, recovery, and every stage of therapy. Maybe capturing these moments gave me a sense of what I hoped to become history. *She is going to get better and here is where you were.*

Celebrating the smallest of improvements brought back memories of her very first steps, learning to ride a bicycle, standing on snow skis, and sitting up in the saddle of a horse so big that she could hardly get her little legs over the horse, and not even be close to touching the stirrups.

Now, new challenges, new territory, which was so much more important and impactful to the quality of Heather's life. *We can do this. We can help her, and she will overcome these limitations. She is strong, tenacious, and God will use this to help others. He told me she is going to have a "wonderful life." I know she will.*

Along with my photo journaling of her associated physical and occupational therapies, I was writing frequent emails to friends and family with a subject line of: "Heather Updates." The purpose was to allow us to stay focused on taking care of Heather by communicating with all those interested in her situation. I always ended those emails with requests for continued prayers for Heather and us. We have created an Appendix here: "Heather Updates," with all the notes to give you a real time perspective of what was going on with her during this period.

When we realized that our medical insurance coverage for therapy was going to run far short of her immediate needs, I thought we better investigate getting her additional financial support to help cover all her therapy needs. As the marketing guy, I estimated the shortfall requirements, developed a plan to touch people concerning Heather's needs, and executed a campaign titled, "Heather's Fight For Therapy," featuring boxing gloves, prompted from a story to Heather from our lead pastor/boxer the night before her surgery. We gave her those in the hospital and had anyone involved, from her surgery through therapy, sign them, showing support for her long-term efforts.

We built a website with a video telling Heather's story and

requesting financial support and prayers, as well as holding a fund-raising event featuring dinner at a restaurant with the finest view of Pittsburgh, wine tasting, live music, a celebrity master of ceremonies, and guest speakers.

The response of prayers, donations, and support were overwhelming. Generosity of family and friends truly saved the day. Thank you all.

The Champion

I was attending out-patient therapy three days a week and doing my exercises at home with my mom. We mastered a daily routine of transfers to and from my wheelchair, showering, and therapy exercises. I liked to call my mom my "left-hand man." I didn't need a right-hand man since my right hand worked just fine, but I was in desperate need for a left-hand man and my mom was the perfect candidate for the job. We worked well together, and I found myself enjoying the closeness with my mom.

It was much like I had regressed back into a child, dependent on her for my basic needs. However, the strong will inside me kept reminding me this was not the way it was supposed to be; I was made to be an independent woman. This powerful will inside me gave me the motivation I needed to keep pushing, keep trying.

I was fortunate to get two therapists at the out-patient rehab with the same first name, Josh. My dad joked that they knew I had brain surgery and wanted to make things easy on me. Both Joshes were fantastic. Clearly, they were extremely knowledgeable, and just nice down-to-earth people. These are qualities every therapist should have, since your patients are experiencing a horrible time in their life and just need patience, support, and respect. Both PT Josh and OT Josh were examples of that.

They also appreciated my humor. I have always been a person to crack jokes or try and make light of a heavy situation. I remember one day in particular; I was doing a therapy exercise where they strapped my left hand to a steering wheel and I had to steer it only using my left hand. It was a rather big steering wheel, and I said I was driving a school bus "full of Polish children." We all laughed and it was a brief

73

moment of joy.

Therapy was tough; you put in all this time and effort but only see minimal results. Recovering from a brain injury is like watching grass grow. If you sit and stare at your lawn, you won't notice the growth, however, if you give it time and then take a look, it will have grown immensely. It is rather frustrating to be patient when it is your mobility and quality of life you are waiting for. How did I stay motivated to keep working at it? I just put my focus on wanting to run again or ride my horse again. These things were unjustly taken from me and I was going to do everything in my power to get them back.

The out-patient rehab gave me credit for my attitude towards my recovery and awarded me the Champion Award of the facility. They gave a very sweet nomination speech, highlighting not only my shown dedication to my recovery, but also how I did it all with a smile on my face and found humor through the pain. What an honor! It was not only a proud moment in my recovery, but it also was motivation to keep going with my optimistic attitude.

When the road looks rough and uncertain, just put your mind on what you want, and let those desires push you each and every day. If your loved one was in danger, you would most likely do anything to fight for them and save them, right? Why not fight for yourself? We so often put others before ourselves and forget our self-worth. You need to fight for YOU! That is exactly what I was doing, fighting for me. The thoughts of running and riding a horse again flooded my brain and kept me focused. I was sure of it, I was going to make a full recovery and be just the same as before! *All I have to do is keep fighting.*

As I gained a little more mobility, such as walking short distances and being able to dress myself one handed, I got to start doing more things. I remember one weekend, Greg asked me to go away with him to a summer home he had by a lake. I was very excited to get away and have some alone time with my fiancé, but then reality struck. *How romantic will this be when Greg has to help bathe me and take care of me like I am a helpless child? Will he call off the wedding?* I was devastated with emotion. Why can't things be like they were before? Greg and I used to go to this summer place all the time before my stroke/brain surgery, and had many wild and carefree nights. But now everything had changed. Throughout my recovery I was very focused on the end goal and tried not to dwell on the negative things or thoughts. I tried to focus on the things I could do and not think about the stuff I couldn't do, although there were times I had no choice but to recognize my inability to do certain things. A 23-year-old should be able to just go away with her fiancé and be excited about a romantic weekend. This was not the case for me.

We decided to just do a one-night stay instead of the whole weekend, since it was my first time "away." It was a beautiful time together. Oh, how my fears were irrational! I ended up having my first glass of wine since before everything happened, and after only about two sips I was pretty tipsy and slurring my words. Greg was worried that something was wrong, but I giggled and assured him I was just fine and must have now become a cheap drunk. *Oh, how this was different from our college days, Greg!*

Our little getaway had me even more excited for our wedding. Greg was so special, he was supportive, made me laugh, and now I could see he would stick with me through "sickness and health." We started working hard on planning our wedding and looking at venues. There was a Catholic church we used to drive past each of the hundreds of times we went to the hospital when I was having bleeds. It was gorgeous and Greg really wanted to get married in a Catholic church. I wasn't Catholic, but would do that, since it was so important to him. While looking for venues we were looking for something beautiful yet charming. One thing I didn't feel was beautiful, as I hobbled around with a leg brace and a cane. But we found the perfect place. It was a hotel in downtown Pittsburgh, and the wedding planner also had brain surgery! It was a match made in heaven.

My walking was slowly improving. I was starting to walk without my cane and not fall over. I had to use a leg brace to walk, but had no cane. I was making progress! My vision of walking down the aisle to marry Greg was looking like a real possibility. My left hand was slowly improving, but the changes were not as drastic. I kept working though, knowing one day I was going to be just the same as I was before, if I only keep trying. My hand was the hardest to work in therapy. Due to really bad spasticity in my muscles, my left hand was always in a tight fist and I could not open my hand on my own. We tried different stretches to try and loosen the muscles, but it seemed that nothing was working. When I would get really frustrated, my hand would get stiffer, a lose/lose situation. So, I developed a mantra to help relax, I said, "Aruba, Aruba, Aruba," which made me think of my favorite place in the world, dream of drinking a beer with my left hand, with a Cuban cigar in my right. After a follow up appointment, my doctor recommended Botox injections. You read that right, Botox injections.

Botox is typically used to help prevent wrinkles, but in my case, it would help my hand not be in a tight fist all the time. The Botox would be injected directly into my muscle that was spastic; after a couple weeks, it would paralyze that muscle so it wouldn't be firing all the time. Sounded a little scary, but I was desperate. *Maybe my left arm will look young and wrinkle free forever.*

The Botox gave me false hope that it would magically make my hand work like before. I am not sure where I got that thought, but that is not what happened. It certainly helped the stiffness, but my brain was still having trouble recognizing my hand was still there. Although this was highly frustrating, since my hand was not working as well as my leg, I really learned how to adapt living one-handed in a two-handed world. I remember the day I first learned how to put deodorant on under both arms and it was exciting. I thought, *I may be one-handed, but at least I won't stink!*

Then reality struck again. I was getting ready to take a break from out-patient therapy and just do my exercises at home, since I was totally worn out. On my last day of therapy, before my break, my one Josh was taking measurements and I was getting frustrated at what little use of my hand I still had. I asked him bluntly, "Do you think I will ever regain full use of my left hand?" He said no, he did not think I would ever regain full use again. I was totally crushed and devastated. How could he crush my hopes and dreams like that? I cried for what seemed like days. *Up until this moment, I was sure I would gain full use of everything again, but now I am doubting everything.*

Honestly, this was a huge turning point for me. While at first I was mad at Josh for saying this to me, I appreciate his honesty now. This forced me to accept the fact that this was my life now, and that was okay. I had two options, either give up, or be happy with what I can do and learn how to live the fullest life I can within my abilities. I could walk again, which was a massive accomplishment, and my left hand worked enough to help with certain things. It was time to adapt to life as it was, not as I wished it was.

Isn't that what life is all about? It is a constant ride of adapting to our situations. As we talked about before, there is the picture we thought our life would look like, and then there is the reality. Life never goes as planned, so we must either give up or adapt to the curve balls. Did you plan on being married and with children by age 25? But now you are single at 35? You have two options: Either give up, or you can adapt and stay hopeful that your future husband is out there, and maybe you will adopt. Did you expect to have your dream job and career by the time you were 30? But you are stuck at a dead-end job and can't seem to find your dream job? Well, you have two options: You can either give up on your dream job, or you can adapt and stay optimistic that your dream job will come, and maybe you are just gaining more experience to add to your resume. It all comes down to you! Believe me, I know it can be hard to just give up on your life picture, but if you adapt, you will learn to make the best of it. Boy, was my life a lot different than I had wanted it to be.

I may have started to accept the fact that my life would never be the same, but I was still working hard at therapy. Maybe I could prove Josh wrong. I had a new plan in my mind. I was going to get through my recovery and go live the "wonderful life" God told my dad I was going to live. I already dealt with my fair share of life's disappointments, right? You guessed it; I was wrong. My journey was not yet over.

Mom Here

This was a very interesting period for me. As I had mentioned, I worked at a rehabilitation facility in my professional life. I actually worked at the one Heather was attending for out-patient therapy. I was on the spinal cord team, and that pod was located right beside the out-patient therapy area. I was now on the other side of the desk, a family member of a patient. It was a weird self-evaluating moment. *Did I really do my job well back then? When I counseled family members, did the advice I gave help or was it patronizing?*

On that very first day, the physical therapist evaluated Heather.

One of those tests was being able to pick up a pencil off floor from a standing position. She was not able to do that, and my heart broke once again for her. To see your child struggle to complete the simplest of tasks was a hard thing to watch. *OK, Mom, what did you tell families who tried to do everything for their children they couldn't do? "You need to allow them to struggle to regain whatever independence is possible. That will give them the confidence they need to figure it out. To adapt to their new situation, this is the new normal. I know this is a very hard thing to watch, but this is their life now and I am sure you want them to live it well." OK, I get it, I may not like it, but I get it.*

God gave us free will. I could choose to look at my daughter's struggles and feel sorry for her, or I could look at her strength and determination, and admire her courage. Now I am not going to lie and say I always looked at her situation that way. I am human after all. However, I did try, and in a weird way, my former career provided me with some insights to believe that was true.

Dad Here

Heather in a wheelchair was a big struggle for me. It made me sad and frustrated, because I often didn't know how to help. *Was I going to bang her into something? Take too long to get her to a bathroom?* Due to her determination and very hard work, she overcame the need for that wheelchair.

The two therapists named Josh reminded me of a TV sitcom, "Newhart," where the one character would always introduce himself, "I'm Larry. This is my brother Darryl, and this is my other brother Darryl." I would always think Heather should wheel around in her wheelchair with her two therapists and introduce herself, saying, "Hi, I'm Heather. This is my therapist Josh and this is my other therapist Josh."

I truly loved and respected these therapists. They were both sincerely dedicated to helping Heather improve and regain function. Something I struggled with, just wanting to help her get better was that they pushed her and encouraged her to keep moving and trying new things. That is what she did. Walking further and further down the halls. Up and down stairs in a stairwell, finally walking the entire distance of the huge rehab facility, and on her last day walking out the front door. Never gave up. Adjusted to her circumstances to make the best of what she had.

Her strokes and brain surgery were certainly not what I wanted for my daughter. She was a fit athlete. That was taken away, however, I needed to adjust also. If she was not going to stop working and striving to improve, I needed to be the most supportive dad, I could be, always watching for opportunities to make things more accessible and comfortable for her.

I am a very creative person and have full faith that God is going to guide us and support us. He did.

The Great Leap

The break from out-patient therapy was much needed. No, I wasn't just giving up on my recovery, I was still doing exercises at home, just not going to the rehabilitation center. I was walking without assistance and was focusing on regaining more use of my left hand. I needed a break from going to the center every day, just to focus on living my life as normally as possible.

Greg and I were blessed that his grandfather sold us his house in Pittsburgh for a very reasonable price. This would give us the leg up we needed to start our marriage off on a good foot. We were now only months away from the wedding. All the planning seemed to be coming together.

Greg went away one weekend with his guy friends and I got an unexpected call in the middle of the night that Greg had fallen off a cliff. Apparently, they were walking through a field and he thought he could just hop over some rocks. Little did he know, there was a ditch on the other side of those rocks. Greg fell almost ten feet and landed on his face, shattering many bones. There was obviously alcohol involved; that definitely led to the impairment of judgment. It was a miracle he was alive and had zero brain damage, but he would now need extensive reconstructive surgery to his face. Not to forget, we were scheduled to get married soon.

The hospital closest to the accident was about two hours away from home, so my mom and I drove out there in the middle of the night. Greg looked horrible, but he was conscious and alert. My main concern was finding him a qualified surgeon to put his face back together. The surgeon we saw at the hospital was young and made a comment while reviewing the scans, "I've never seen something like this before." Not the kind of thing you want a surgeon saying about your fiancé's face. So, we ended up having Greg transferred to a hospital closer to home for his care. What did they do? They made an appointment with a plastic surgeon and released him to go home.

I spent the night with him that night he was first home, because the only thing holding his eyeball in his head was all the swelling in his face; he had shattered all the bones that formed his eye socket. That was a rather sleepless night, as I monitored his breathing and made sure his eyeball didn't fall out. The next day, we went to the appointment with the plastic surgeon. As we entered his office, full of breast implant samples and nose job pictures, I knew we were not in the right place. The young, good-looking plastic surgeon wearing snakeskin boots came in, looked at Greg's face, and said, "That's disgusting; you need to clean that up." We politely declined any further consult and left the office.

Fortunately, I got a call one day from a representative at UPMC, the hospital where my brain surgery was performed. The caller asked if I would star in a commercial for them. They wanted to highlight the advanced technology they used for my surgery. I enthusiastically accepted the opportunity, and it was a once-in-a-lifetime experience. We filmed eight hours for a 60-second commercial. I felt like a celebrity every time I saw it on television.

When Greg needed surgery on his face, I reached out to the representative from the UPMC commercial for help, and she graciously got us in to see a surgeon right away. In addition, they were able to do the procedure the next day, so they admitted Greg into the hospital. I was so relieved I wouldn't have to be on "eyeball watch" anymore.

Greg had the surgery and everything went well, thank God. The miracle was, Greg's face looked exactly like it did before the fall. We were back on track as the power couple we were.

Between my unfortunate health issues and Greg's shattered face, we were certainly made for each other. Greg loved me during a time when most young men would have run away in fear. I returned that love when he fell like Humpty Dumpty. Were things perfect in our relationship? No, but we clearly loved each other through thick and thin, so that's all that mattered. Or so I thought...

Remember my passion for riding horses? Since I was unable to ride using two hands, that meant I could not ride English like before, but I was desperate to find a way to get back in the saddle. What is a riding style that only requires the use of one hand? You guessed it, Western. But me being me, I either go big or go home. This time I did not pick just Western, but barrel racing. Oh, my poor parents. I found a barn north of where my parents lived and an instructor who was patient enough to work with me, given my limitations. She put me on a horse named Murphy, who was just as patient. Barrel racing was so much different from hunter/jumpers, so we took things slow until I learned the new discipline.

I was so happy to be in the saddle again and to feel that "riding sore" feeling once again. No, it was not the same as before, but it was close, and I had to be thankful for that. My disability quickly reminded me that my riding days were over, however, when the horse I was riding took off galloping and my left-sided weakness caused me to fall off. In the past, I had the leg strength and balance to stay on in almost any situation, but my disability prevented me from that now. I fell to the ground, and at first, I thought I was fine, but then came excruciating pain in my left arm. I was, in fact, not fine, but sat screaming, crying in my mom's car while she drove me to the emergency room. X-rays would show I had managed to fracture my arm in not one, but TWO places. All I was hoping for was to not have the cast on for my wedding in a few months.

This injury made me rethink my plan of riding again, post-stroke and brain surgery. *Maybe I needed to hang up my riding helmet for good, before I injure myself anymore.* So how did I deal with the reality of ending my riding? It was hard to accept; I felt like my world was ending. I think I had loved horses so much it had become part of my identity. It was literally who I was as a person. I was a girl who rode horses and worked hard, so she could ride more horses. But now I could no longer be that girl. In that case, who was I? This was when I started referring to the pre-stroke and brain surgery self as the "old Heather." She was now dead, and the "new Heather" was born and needed to figure out what her life would look like and who she was as a person. So far, she had overcome a stroke and brain surgery, regained her ability to walk, and was about to get married. Her life was just beginning.

While I could walk without assistance, my walking was very rough and I often tripped, since spasticity gave me such trouble picking up my left set of toes. Spasticity happens when the connection between the brain and spinal cord is damaged, thus making your muscles on the affected side very tight. My one doctor recommended I see an orthopedic surgeon to inquire about tendon-lengthening surgery. The doctor I was referred to thought he could greatly improve my walking with tendon-lengthening surgery on my Achilles tendon and foot. I was so excited for the results, and thought this could be what lets me run again. Now that riding was out of my future, maybe running could replace it. I had such high hopes, because my lack of mobility had made me gain weight and I was starting to not like the girl I saw in the mirror. But running had made me so fit before. This was my last hope.

I had the tendon-lengthening surgery and was put in a cast until the tendons healed enough that it could be taken off. This surgery was slightly frustrating, because it took me backward in my recovery. Due to the cast and just weakness from the procedure, I was unable to walk up or down stairs, so I stayed at my parents' house where there was a bathroom on the first floor and got to experience the joys of sleeping on the couch.

While it was frustrating to be back at this level of incapacity, I was focusing on how this surgery was going to improve my walking and overall quality of life. I already felt like my walking, despite the cast, was immensely improved. Like I have stated before, all you've got to do is keep your focus on the end goal. I have always loved the analogy that, just like a bow and arrow, *"An arrow can only be shot by pulling it backward. When life is dragging you back with difficulties, it means it's going to launch into something great. So just focus, and keep aiming."*

Now think of what you're striving to obtain right now. Think of what you've endured, failed, and had mini success through. The longer you can hold onto the bowstring, and the further back you can pull it, will determine the trajectory of your success. It takes time, commitment, strength, action, and a mindset that is infallible.

Success is difficult; long-term success is even harder. You have to find that place where you can keep digging and constantly be moving forward. Every disappointment, every mini-failure, every hiccup in the road of your journey, pulls that arrow back further and further. It's just a matter of time or, if you like numbers, it keeps increasing the probability of success. You're nearly there. Don't give up and don't forget why you started in the first place. If you just stop now, what was the point? Don't give up on your dream. Don't give those people who said you're ridiculous and your dreams are too big the satisfaction of saying, "I told you so."

After months of healing, I finally got the cast off and was able to start physical therapy. Oh, how happy I was with the results. My walking had greatly improved and my limp became much less noticeable. Now I started to focus on the next big-ticket item, my left hand. Despite the Botox injections, my left hand was still always in a tight fist. This was uncomfortable; my nails continuously dug into my palm and it was obviously hard to use my hand when it was clenched in a ball. Not to forget, it was quite noticeable to other people that something wasn't quite right. The surgeon who performed the tendon-lengthening surgery on my foot referred me to another surgeon who could do the same procedure, but on my hand. I got it scheduled, but made sure to do it after the wedding, of course.

Then the big day came. Greg and I had our wedding and it was perfect. We had the ceremony in a gorgeous Catholic church and the reception at an upscale downtown Pittsburgh hotel. As I was walking down the aisle toward my future husband, I was beyond excited. Not only was I going to marry this man who had stood by my side throughout this time, but I was walking! I had worked so very hard for so very long. It was a beautiful fall day and all our guests seemed to have a wonderful time. The physical therapist from my outpatient therapy was there, and I found out he had been so inspired by my story that he wanted to see it to completion. One very special moment was when my neurosurgeon and his wife attended the wedding, also. I saved one dance just for him and we danced to "I Hope You Dance©," written by Mark Sanders and Tia Sillers, and sung by Lee Ann Womak. Everyone in the room lost it with that, and everyone was clapping and cheering. Greg enjoyed himself as well, even so much that he fell asleep in the bathroom of our honeymoon suite, while I got to enjoy the big king-sized bed by myself. All right, not everything was perfect about that day, but it was pretty darn close!

I guess I could finish the book here and say I lived happily ever after, but that would be a lie. I did have more challenges to face, but I did not know it yet.

Mom Here

The barrel racing incident was so Heather. At the wedding, her neurosurgeon noticed she was holding her arm differently and asked me about it. When I told him, she had fractured it in two places when she was learning how to barrel race, he just shook his head and laughed.

Funny story about the trip to the hospital the night Greg fell off the cliff. Heather had been caring for Roxy, a large female Doberman. When she woke me up to tell me about Greg, and I knew she couldn't yet make that drive on her own, I asked my husband if he wanted to take her and I would watch Roxy, or should I take Heather and he would care for the dog. Randy was not actually a dog lover, he liked them, but was not a big fan. He said I should take Heather, and if he had to leave the house, he would put Roxy in her crate. So off we went. The next morning, I called home to check on Randy and Roxy, only to find out that he had put her in her crate, but when he came home, he found the crate in pieces and Roxy, happy as a clam, laying on the couch with a big wet toy in her mouth. Oops.

Greg had his surgery and we were getting ready for the wedding. The "save the dates" went out and had a picture of two hockey helmets with the wording, "Save the date before it's too late." Heather and Greg now had matching scars on their skulls. The wedding was so joyous and love filled the room. We were celebrating life and the two lives we could have lost. I thanked God many times for the blessings he had given us.

Life is precious and these two human beings could have easily not made it to this beautiful day. Life may be hard right now, but please appreciate the small things every day... a flower, a thunderstorm, lightening bugs, or the sound of crickets. We never know when that day will be our last.

Dad Here

When I first heard about Heather wanting to ride Western, I

85

thought to myself, *over these years of living with my wife and two daughters I often kept thoughts to myself.* I distinctly remember thinking, *Western riding, are you nuts? Oh, barrel racing, now I know this brain surgery has affected Heather's and her mom's mental capacities.*

On the day of her falling off the horse and breaking her arm in two places, I was driving back from a business appointment where a client had accepted a very big opportunity for my business. It was a beautiful day and I was really feeling good. Then the cell phone rang and Lynn told me she was at the emergency room. *Who? What? How? Were my questions.* "You have got to be kidding me!!!" (Response). *I am not sure I can handle any more of this,* was my thought. *Ok, Randy pray for peace and understanding.* "Lord, help Heather. Heal Heather. Help me to understand and accept that she is just testing her limitations and for me to be sympathetic and supportive of her.*

When she told me she was considering more surgeries, all I could think was, *has she not been through enough?* I have no experience in this, I have never broken anything or had major surgery. If she is willing, and the doctors feel it will help her, then go for it. *I love you very much and am sad that you are going through this.* Yet, I was, and am, so very proud of her strength and determination to improve and regain as much as possible.

Wedding day. Walking Heather down the spiral staircase in our home where she was born. This remains one of my fondest memories; I still carry the photo of the two of us coming down the stairs together in my briefcase. There were many times prior to that I was not sure she would physically be able to do this trip down 24 steps. But we did and she was beautiful.

Saint Paul's Cathedral in Pittsburgh has the world's longest center aisle anywhere. (Maybe it just felt that way). As we were walking down the aisle together, all I could feel was the love of all those attending the service. Yes, she was a beautiful bride, but she gracefully walked down that long aisle, holding my arm. After the service and everyone had left for the reception, Heather and I had a moment at the church altar, kneeling and praising God for blessing her with the ability to walk again.

The New Beginning

The wedding was over and Greg and I were starting our life together in our own home. I had scheduled the next tendon-lengthening surgery for my left hand and successfully graduated from college with my bachelor's degree. Not only did I graduate, but graduated *magna cum laude* of my class. I was so proud and honestly relieved I was able to accomplish such a goal, despite having a stroke and brain surgery.

I started my career by working part-time for the company my parents owned. Part-time was necessary, since I was still dealing with immense fatigue from my brain injury. It was nice to work for my family and have the flexibility in my schedule when needed. There were days I had to leave early or work from home, due to the sleepless nights. These nights were due to Greg having friends over to our house late at night and into the wee hours of the morning. We were the only people in his group of friends to own a house, so we were the destination of the festivities and the free hotel for said friends to crash. We also lived in walking distance to bars, so there was that factor, as well.

While I tried to understand and be a "go with the flow" wife, I knew, deep down, this sort of lifestyle of constant flows of people in and out of our house was not normal. I would voice my concerns to Greg, but he never seemed to understand my side of things. On one hand, Greg's friends were more like family. He couldn't change the fact his work schedule was different than mine, and the only time he had to see his friends was on my work nights. But on the other hand, did spending time with friends always have to include binge drinking and going to bars until the early morning hours? I knew I wasn't being completely irrational, but we needed to find a way to make this work.

When my dad decided to sell his company and try the retired life, I was left without a job. Fortunately, Greg made enough money to support us while I found a job. I was able to find another part-time position and Greg and I started seeing a marriage counselor. Greg was very hesitant and reluctant to go with me, which led to many arguments. Having experience with therapy, I could tell the therapist we were seeing was pretty unorthodox in his methods. We ended up only having a few sessions before I decided we were not benefitting from it. Just like any medical professional, either you fit with them or not.

In a nutshell, married life was not all I had hoped and dreamed it would be. Maybe that is the case for everyone at first, but it was hard. There were nights Greg would go out with his friends and not come home. Then we would have a very serious conversation about these events and things would get better for a couple of months. *Maybe we can do this!*

I had my left-hand surgery and, although it was a painful recovery, I was thrilled with the results. My left hand was no longer in a tight fist, but open! I couldn't really use the fingers, but at least it was open. The next procedure was eye surgery to help improve the double vision I'd had since the surgery. Apparently, the brain damage affected the tendons attached to my eye, as well, so those needed to be lengthened. *Add it to the list, Heather!*

So, after recovering from the hand surgery, I was faced with surgery on my left eye. Much like the foot and hand, the tendons in my eye were over-reacting and would cause double vision, among other problems. They lengthened the tendons to my eye, and it was a fairly easy recovery. I remember being so fed up with all these surgeries. I did not ask for all of this. All I wanted to do was move on from the stroke and brain surgery, but my spastic tendons wanted me to remember. Once again, I had to reshape my focus and focus on the end goal. These corrective surgeries would give me at least a little bit of normalcy in life, or so I hoped.

Life is hard. I think, so often when we go through hard times, we think, "This is it. No more hard times for me, I've met my quota." However, that is not how life works. You will go through multiple hard times, some more severe than others, but they are going to keep happening to you. Dark, huh? Well, unfortunately it happens and you either break or learn from it. What if each of these hard times is trying to teach us something? Life is all about the experiences, the good and the bad. Hard times are just bad experiences, but they shape us and our lives in some form. Life happens. News flash, none of us are getting out of here alive.

Greg and I decided to start trying to have a baby, but when evaluating our surroundings in preparation, we decided to move first. The house was great, but in a bad area of town and not quite big enough for a growing family. Luckily, it sold in just 48 hours, and we quickly found our dream home. It was at the top of our price range, but was utterly perfect. Jut stepping foot in the house, I could envision Greg and I with our kids, but since it was at the top of our price range, I needed to find a full-time job to help pay the mortgage.

Then began my anxiety. How would I start a full-time position? As mentioned before, I suffer from extreme fatigue and need more sleep than the average person. How would I work and get up every morning to go to work again? How would I manage doing all the household chores on top of my daily job? These thoughts ran through my mind and caused me to have a very serious conversation with Greg to come up with a plan. I explained to him that me working full time was going to require him to step up and help out more around the house. He was in agreement and indicated that he would help out more, especially on his days off. So that was it, we bought our dream home.

This house was perfect. It was in a great school district, close to family, and had ample space for babies. So, once I came off my birth control, we started trying to have a child. Growing up, I always thought having a child would happen instantaneously. Boy, was I wrong? We tried and tried, following all the guidelines and tips we could find, but to no avail. Each month was full of hope and excitement, followed by disappointment and tears. Was it me? Was it Greg? I couldn't figure out a clear explanation. I only got more and more discouraged and frustrated.

Then I landed my full-time job in the field I went to college for, human resources! The very special part of this job was it was with an organization that helped people with disabilities. Obviously, being a woman with a physical disability, it was very special for me to be helping others. However, how would I be able to work a full-time job with this brain injury of mine? Although the fear was there, I knew I had no choice. It took a little time to adjust, and lots of coffee, but I did it and felt so empowered.

Greg and I continued to have issues at home. His friends were his family, but sometimes I felt like I was just a roommate who got the job of cleaning up after him and his friends. This just didn't feel right. When we would talk about my feelings of under appreciation, he would say I was just nagging and things would change when we had a baby. Each month came with another negative pregnancy test. I was starting to feel like it was never going to happen. *After everything I've been through, why can't God give me this blessing of having a child?*

Things between Greg and me became more and more challenging, so the baby-trying got put on the back burner. I did not want to have a child unless Greg and I were in a good, solid place. At that time, I felt our relationship was very one-sided; I was putting in all the effort and Greg was not stepping up to the plate. Marriage is supposed to be a partnership and I felt something was missing in mine. Greg was not too excited about the break we were taking in trying for a baby, but I had to stick to my gut.

We decided to put the focus on our relationship and start seeing a new marriage therapist. Greg was much more willing to go this time, so I was very hopeful this would start to solve our problems. However, the one-sided relationship continued and left me even more confused. The therapist would give us homework to do between sessions, but I felt I was the only one doing them. Maybe Greg did not know how to complete the assignment, and I wished he had reached out to me for help. Greg was very open and engaged in our sessions, but once we left, it felt like nothing was different.

Our new, hopefully future home was constantly full of Greg's friends; the other nights, Greg would go out and not come home until the early hours of the morning. As I've said, Greg's friends were his family and I empathized about how important spending time with them was to him. While I would rather not have had my husband go to bars, I was relieved to not have a mess to clean up, or people sleeping on my floor. I felt, when I tried to explain my feelings to Greg, he was hearing them, but they were not registering.

Then I had an epiphany. I started questioning if I wanted to have kids. This struck me as a shock, because ever since I was young, becoming a mother had always been a dream of mine. After some soul searching, I realized it was not that I did not want to have children, but it just did not feel like it was meant to happen with Greg. Wow! I then had to really ponder why I was feeling this way.

Once I figured out why I was questioning having kids, I had a very serious conversation with Greg as a last-ditch effort. At first, Greg seemed responsive to how I was unhappy and things needed to change, but within 24 hours of our conversation, Greg became closed off and angry. He could not understand why I was unhappy, since he did not physically abuse me and he provided a nice life for us. All of this was true, but I needed more out of a marriage and I wanted to work on improving things together. Greg quickly indicated to me that he was not willing to change things, and I was being unreasonable.

After a week of hard thinking and a lot of tears, I felt that if Greg wasn't willing to try and work on our marriage, then it was time to call it quits after four years of trying everything possible. *Oh my goodness! First brain surgery, and now a divorce?*

I was very saddened and overwhelmed, but deep down my gut was telling me I was making the right decision. My willpower was tested when I would think of the last eight years we'd spent together. Although there were bad memories, there were also so many good memories. What a love story we had together. We overcame so much, and stuck by each other's sides through everything, but even the unbreakable can fall.

Greg is an amazing person. He is funny, caring, and kind. I do not wish him any ill will, only happiness. The fun, heartwarming memories of us together, I will carry with me always.

Mom Here

Heather and I had spent so much time side-by-side over the last year and a half, helping her after her brain bleeds, brain surgery, rehabilitation, and daily living activities, that those Momma Bear instincts were in full force again. There were times during her marriage that I believed Greg was not being as helpful as I thought he should be, but I told myself maybe that is because he doesn't see her as disabled.

Heather's tenacity enabled her to fight through any challenge. I was aware of the "buddy family" because of Greg losing his dad at a young age, and his buddies did step up and help him.

After all, he had stood by Heather through five strokes and brain surgery; he must love her. Initially, he was willing to go to marriage counseling, so I was hopeful. I guess I felt he just needed to mature and realize that Heather was his family now. I did know about some of the drinking, but not to what extent it was happening. I encouraged Heather to continue to work on the marriage.

My husband and I have been married for 40 years, and believe me, there have been rough patches. That is what I thought this was with Heather and Greg.

When Heather told me they had decided to divorce, my heart broke for my daughter, once again. She had been through so very much. In addition, she was still going through surgery after surgery to enable her to live her life. I felt badly for Greg, also. He was a good guy with a good heart, but I guess Heather's expectation of a partnership was different than his. As Heather said, I also wish him the best and I hold no ill will toward him.

I know Heather was disappointed that the baby didn't happen, but once again, I saw God in this. The divorce and starting a new life would have had so many more challenges. The other blessing was the willingness of both parties to make it fast and simple. Heather mourned the loss of her marriage, but in true Heather fashion, she said," Okay, let's move forward." Their dream home sold very quickly, and by a weird coincidence or blessing, she fell in love with the house of the folks who bought hers. Her new life had begun.

Having children is not for the faint of heart. Any parent realizes that when they first put that little bundle in your arms, you just need to buckle your seat belt, enjoy the ride, and know God can get you through anything. It may take a while, but with His help, you will figure it out.

Dad Here

So very proud of Heather's determination to go back to school and to finish so strong, graduating *magna cum laude* was amazing.

Regarding her working for me, I was so glad that I could help Heather get started with research and writing work that she could do when she could and when she was able. I was very concerned about her ability to maintain a "Big Girl Job" in her field of human resource management, because of her lack of stamina at the time.

I gave her an office across from mine and often saw her door closed and the lights out. My heart went out to her. I didn't know if this was going to be her new normal or if she would gain strength and stamina over time.

I did look forward to lunch time. Her mom and I worked together in our business, and of course Heather would organize a lunch meeting in my office each day to give the three of us an uninterrupted time to talk and get caught up. She always seemed to perk-up for these lunches, so I looked forward to them. It truly gave me a glimmer of hope that she was still my little Heather, and she was going to be fine.

As I am reading this, I honestly forgot about Heather's eye surgery. As soon as I read her note about it, I remembered the pre-evaluations and assorted exams to determine if she was a good candidate for this surgery and how it may help her. It is not that I thought less of this surgery than any of the others. There have just been so many I had lost track of the eye surgery.

I am so thankful that God did not provide Heather the baby she was trying so hard for. I believe God is the Creator of all life and He knows better than any of us that this was not her time.

When Heather was a little girl, she often told Lynn and me, "When I was in heaven, I picked you as my parents." Well, I believe there is a little girl or boy looking down from heaven at Heather and thinking, when it is the right time, Heather is going to be my mommy.

When Heather informed us of her decision to get a divorce, I was very sad, yet I had felt for a very long time she was not happy. She was not herself; as a dad, you just want your daughter to be happy, healthy, cared for, and loved.

The Phoenix

The divorce hit me pretty hard, obviously. I had been through so much with Greg, and truly felt we could get through anything. I guess some things are just not meant to be.

Greg moved out of our dream house, which made things official; this was happening. We agreed to do things simply and cut it down the middle. It felt so weird to be having these types of conversations with someone I thought I was spending the rest of my life with. Although it was uncomfortable, I appreciated Greg's ability to make things as civil as possible.

But what does my life look like without Greg? How will I afford to live on my own? Will I ever be loved again? Will I find someone who loves me, despite my disability? These were all questions and fears running through my head. I had spent almost ten years of my life with Greg, and he was with me through some of the darkest moments of my life. Yes, there were bad times, but there were also some really good times we shared together. I was going to have to mourn the relationship, as if there was a death. Fortunately, I had friends and parents who helped me immensely through the process, whether it was just letting me vent, hugging me while I cried, or just lending a helping hand. I was very fortunate to have this sort of support in this transition.

We put the dream house on the market and I continued to live in it while Greg was living with his mom. At no surprise to me, we got multiple offers on the house within days. I loved this house and everything it encompassed. It was beautiful, big, and where I pictured having my first child. Now it was time for it to bring joy to another family. I was sad it sold so quickly, but also relieved, since that meant it was time I could start looking for my next house.

If you haven't noticed already, I tend to just get up and go, no matter what the situation. When faced with difficult times, I buckle up and get through it. Couldn't we all try and do that? When something hard hits you, just brush it off and get going. Life goes on, with or without us, so why not just keep moving forward with it? This was not how I pictured my life to go, at all. First a stroke and brain surgery, and now a divorce. But what I remember when I get frustrated with my various detours in life is this: When a road you drive on every day to work goes under construction and closes, it's highly frustrating. There is a detour route to get you around the closing, but it adds time to your commute and is usually backed up with traffic. You make adjustments, such as leaving a little earlier for work to allow you enough time to take the detour. You make it work. However, after some time, the road is finished, your original route opens up, and you can return to your normal routine. All the construction on the road has made significant improvements. You are ecstatic you have your old route back and it has improved your drive into work. You swear you will never again take this route for granted.

How can we compare this to life? For me, a stroke and brain surgery were a major detour in my life. Then add on the divorce from Greg and you could say my whole life was under major construction. But I made adjustments and took the detour route, since I had no other choice. Yes, this detour was not planned and was frustrating to me, but I decided to just accept the reality and make the best of it. These detours in life help us appreciate things so much better; you just have to be patient and endure.

I was looking at houses left and right. I saw all different kinds. I clearly had a tight budget, but wanted to make sure it was a place where I could envision my future. This was so different than house hunting with Greg. With Greg, I could easily walk into a prospective house and picture us raising a family together. Now my future had no clear picture. Was it just going to be me and the dog in this house? Were there going to be children in this house? There was nothing else I could do but silence my fears and focus again on my new beginning.

The last house I looked at was meant for me. From the moment I pulled up to it on the street, I just knew. It was perfect. Ironically, it was also the house of the people who bought Greg's and my dream house. They were getting a bigger house and I was downsizing. Not going to lie, I was pretty jealous of them and their growing family. It seemed much more desirable than my shrinking one.

Then came Mark. He was hired and started working at the same company I did. The way we started talking was because he had a disability himself; he was hard of hearing. He was so sweet and made me feel like I didn't have a disability of my own. I knew it was not ideal timing, being so close to my divorce, but we do not really control when things happen to us, do we?

We just talked for a while as friends, and then he invited me over to his place for dinner and a movie. He knew about my situation with Greg, and was a patient gentleman to wait until we were officially separated before inviting me over. Even though Greg and I were separated, I still felt weird going on a date with someone else. I had not dated anyone other than Greg for almost 10 years; this was unchartered waters.

Despite my fears, Mark was the perfect gentleman. Just being around him made me forget about everything. I forgot about my disability and the impending divorce. Mark made me feel as if I was a perfect angel who had zero dents or scars and no baggage. I had never felt this way around anyone. How did he do it? We had an indescribable connection to one another. It became obvious to me this was more than a little crush, there was some sort of fate working here. Mark reminded me of a combination of my dad and my grandfather, the two best men I have ever known. Life was beginning to look up.

So, you may be wondering, where am I now? Well, I am happy to report I am living in the house I fell in love with at first sight, and I am engaged to the guy who treats me like a queen! Yes, that is Mark, and we are so happy together and eagerly excited to start this next chapter of our lives together. He is the kindest, most supportive man I have ever known and I am truly lucky.

I am still living one-handed in a two-handed world, but I am excelling in my career and just enjoying life. Yes, I still face struggles, but I still take it on and fight through. I've made it this far, why give up now? I recently found out, due to the limitations on my left side, I have developed pretty severe arthritis in my left foot that will require an intense surgery in the future. Again, not something I had planned for in my life, but I am not going to let it stop me from moving forward and living my best life. But enough about me, let's talk about you.

What did you get from this book? I hope you say it gave you motivation and inspiration to get through whatever life throws at you. Remember, all you have to do today is get up and make your bed. Try just focusing on today and what you can do in this moment. Your plan for your life is not going to happen the way you expected, but you've just got to accept reality and make the most of it; it may turn out better than you expected. Life is going to continuously throw you detours, but just make the adjustments and adapt. You are not in control of what happens to you, but you are in control of how you react to it.

I know you are a fighter; you got this!

Mom Here

I so clearly remember when I found out I was pregnant with Heather; it was a time of great change. We had just moved back to Pittsburgh from Mission Viejo, CA, we were building a house and starting our own business, and now I was pregnant. Just a few major stresses in my life. When I look back on that time, I see that I just decided to take it a day at a time; I knew we would figure it out. We did, and as you have seen in this book, we continue to do so.

Anyone who has raised a child knows it is not for the faint of heart. While I have the blessing of my faith to lean on, know that there have still been dark times. I believe God's vision for me and my family is to depend on Him. God is not working toward a particular finish, just the journey with Him. Heather's journey was so totally out of my "Mom radar" that I could only rely on God to get me through.

I have been so very encouraged by Heather's growth through this trial of life. We all have our things. Life is a journey and can get bumpy at times. Know that there is help out there to get you through. Sometimes, all you need is a caring shoulder to lean on. We are all here to help in any way we can.

Thanks to Heather, we now have a new saying: "Well, at least it's not brain surgery!"

Dad Here

So very proud of Heather to evaluate her situation during a very traumatic time: Where to live and whether to rent or buy, and to do research on the housing market, shop for a mortgage, and invest in real estate all on her own, during what must have felt like a very lonely time. She was not going to let this unfortunate circumstance hold her back. She truly did "get up and go."

Being referred to as one of the best men Heather has ever known is very touching. It is so nice to know she feels this way and it tugs on my heart strings as her Dad.

I am honored to have had the opportunity to be a very small part of this book and Heather's life. It is my sincere hope that God will use Heather's story to challenge you where you need to be challenged, equip you for the limitless opportunities ahead of you, and inspire you to turn your God-given gifts to help others along the way.

Heather Update
(Collection) Appendix

With one of life's surprises, and what would become a life-threatening and life-changing event for my youngest daughter and our family, I felt a need to communicate and keep friends and family informed of what was happening, without direct communications, but with a vehicle that could carry a consistent and timely message. It was one that could be passed along and shared with others, should that be appropriate. I decided on emails with a subject line of "Heather Update."

My goal was threefold:

- To communicate facts as they came available.
- Inform others about any and all upcoming procedures, tests, and what and how Heather was doing.
- Always requesting prayers, because we know God hears our prayers, yet through this very difficult time, realizing that our prayers may not be the best outcome. God wants what is best for us and showed His mercy on Heather. You will see, from the sequence of prayers in these updates, we were praying for no more bleeds. However, her fifth and most serious bleed pushed the cavernous malformation (lesion) to a place where the neurosurgeon was able to remove it, with the least detrimental consequences to Heather, and save her life.

My hope of sharing these notes is to give you a perspective of what Heather was experiencing over a seven-year period, to allow you to walk with Heather and her family from her initial diagnosis through her most recent medical follow-up and MRI results.

Heather Update – March 17, 2012

Friends,

First, I want to thank you all for your continued prayers and support of Heather and our family. Yesterday Heather went through her follow up MRI as planned. The area where she experienced the bleed is continuing to clear. At this point they believe that the cause of the bleed was a Cavernous Malformation which she would have been born with. She continues to recover nicely and I believe she has never looked better physically. She has scheduled another MRI for four months out at the next checkpoint.

Encouraged by her recovery is hampered by my heartbreak for my daughter that now lives with this unfortunate medical issue. I am so very proud of her, her faith in GOD, her strength and courage to not let this hinder her in her life endeavors. As in all of life's challenges Heather is showing all of us how to take every day as the blessing it is and to make the most of every day. To not be concerned about the little inconveniences we encounter, but to step up and make a difference in this thing we all call life. I cannot be more proud of my daughter and I too have committed to her to use her experience as my catalyst to live my life to the fullest. To truly look to Jesus Christ for my guidance and act in accordance.

My hope is that you will continue to pray for Heather that this may never happen to her again and that she continues to recover fully. That she may enjoy the fullness of life and discover GOD's purpose for her life which I believe are great things.

Thank you again,

Randy.

Heather Update – July 14, 2012

Friends,

This week we took Heather to the University of Chicago Neurosurgery Center for her 6-month MRI because they have a specialist that deals with cavernous angioma and one of the most sophisticated MRI's to get the best picture of what is going on. The good news is that Heather only has one of these. The unfortunate news was that it has bled again within the lesion. Not producing as severe physical effects as in December, she is having trouble in reading for long periods, of which she is going to a specialist for testing very soon with hopes that there are some corrective measures that they can help her with.

As I sit here and try to write this note, I struggle. The point of my writing today is to ask for prayers. Now that this has bled again Heather is faced with some life decisions. Does she do nothing, wait, and see if this happens again and risk it being debilitating? Get surgery now and hope that that does not cause any major problems and functions? What doctor, where, when? What about finishing out her senior year in college? Along with many others.

I believe that GOD has a great plan for Heather and that He is only preparing her for great things. My request is for you to continue to pray for Heather to receive Divine guidance to her life and situational questions. That she may enjoy the fulness of life and discover God's purpose for her life.

Thank you very much,

Randy.

Heather Update – July 29, 2012

Friends,

The note below is a Facebook post from Heather, which I believe is a fine update and agree with her decision 100%.

Heather wrote: "I have decided and scheduled to undergo gamma knife surgery to try and prevent my lesion from bleeding again. There are no guarantees it will work, but I trust that God brought me to this decision for a reason. The radiation treatment is scheduled for next Friday and all we can do is put this in His hands and have faith, not fear. I am so blessed to have a family who has supported me through all of this and helped me make the biggest decision of my life. This battle is far from over, but we are strong and we will continue to fight to the best of our ability. With God, all things are possible"

Our continued request for prayers are for a successful outcome and peace. The surgery is scheduled for 6AM on Friday, August 3rd.

Thank you very much,

Randy.

Heather Update – August 3, 2012

Friends,

This morning at 6AM Heather went for her Gamma Knife Surgery. We have been told that all went well and as expected. The good thing about the Gamma Knife Surgery is that it enables the neurosurgeon to treat very small areas of the brain without damaging other vital parts. The unfortunate aspect of the procedure is that it takes a long time for the lesion in this case to be positively affected and prevent future bleeds. The estimates are 18 - 24 months to confirm the results. One surgeon used the analogy of "this is like putting water onto metal and waiting for it to rust." So, we are all praying for our daughter to "rust." In my opinion, this technology is nothing short of a miracle.

Heather is home now and resting. In recovery, she told us, "she felt like someone had hit her with a 2" x 4". The doctors had advised her that the hallo that is used in the procedure would have this effect, but will get better very quickly and she has told us that it has already improved dramatically.

I could not be more proud of my daughter. She has shown incredible courage and strength. Yet what has most impressed me is her faith in God. There is no doubt in my mind that he is using this challenge in her life to prepare her for great things. I have told her that I believe that this procedure will prove to be 100% effective and she will be able to share her experience with many others to help in the future.

Jesus is the great healer and I know he is going to heal Heather for his glory of which we are so thankful for everything. Please continue to pray for Heather and our family as we begin the "rusting process"

Thank you very much,

Randy.

Heather Update – August 12, 2012

Friends,

Heather had experienced some unsettling feelings on Sunday and Monday after her Gamma Knife Surgery (which we were warned that this may be a reaction) to the treatment. So, tomorrow morning at 6:30AM they are going to do another MRI to make sure there is nothing else going on.

Your prayers are greatly appreciated.

Randy.

Heather Update – August 14, 2012

Friends,

As you know Heather had another MRI yesterday and we are so happy to tell you that it did not show any new problems or bleeds.

Thank you, "Jesus."

It is such a relief. Now we wait for the "RUST" (for the Gamma Knife Surgery to do its work).

Our family are all meeting in North Carolina on Saturday for a relaxing vacation and time to unwind from this hectic regiment of doctors' visits and tests. Then Heather is planning on returning to school for the fall semester.

Please continue to pray for her healing and peace. That she may be blessed with total recovery. As well as renewed confidence in all of her skills and abilities. This unfortunate condition had certainly hit her very hard. Yet I can tell you honestly, I have never known a young person with a stronger faith and strength to persevere. I could not be more proud of my daughter.

I will keep you posted periodically on her continued progress.

Thank you all for your prayers and support.

Heather Update – September 19, 2012

Friends,

I wanted to let all of you know that our daughter Heather has been experiencing abnormal symptoms and was admitted to Presbyterian Hospital late yesterday. This morning they told us that her MRI shows another very slight bleed. She is going to be kept overnight again today for observation and treated with a steroid.

We believe that the Gamma Knife Surgery is going to be successful in the long period and we just need to be patient.

Please keep Heather in your prayers as she has been dealt another setback. We place this fully in God's hands because we know that he has this covered and good things for Heather in the future.

Thank you for your continued prayers they are greatly appreciated.

Heather Update – November 12, 2012

Friends,

I have just returned from Presbyterian Hospital and am very sad to tell you that Heather has experienced another small bleed. She has been in school working very hard. She got engaged in early October to Greg, who has been and continues to be by her side and supports and encourages her. We feel very fortunate to be bringing Greg into our family.

Heather is angry, frustrated and scared. All of which I cannot fault her for. We still believe that the Gamma Knife was the right option and know that it will take time (18 to 24 months) to take full effect. We are praying for complete healing.

I ask you to pray for Heather. To give her strength to persevere. Guard her faith that has gotten her this far and will get her through anything. For hope that this too shall pass and that she will be so much stronger of a person for dealing with her challenges that she currently faces. That this will not stop her from graduating from college in the spring and that she does have a very bright and wonderful life ahead. Please pray for Lynn. She has been incredible in these challenges. Ask GOD to give her the strength and wisdom she needs.
Thank you for your continued prayers.

Randy.

Heather Update – November 17, 2012

Friends,

Heather was released from the hospital on Wednesday evening and came home. She did in fact have another small bleed. The doctors have told us that this is unusual, but obviously happens. That the Gamma Knife treatment needs time (18 to 24 months). So, we continue to hope and pray that this does in fact work.

She missed a week of classes this week. She will have off this coming week, which is good so she may continue to rest and recover.

We are asking for continued prayers for Heather's complete healing and that the Gamma Knife Surgery works fully. This has been a big setback for Heather emotionally. She is working so hard at school to get through this semester and still hopes to graduate in the spring. We are praying that her professors will be understanding and work with her so she may meet the needs of her classes. Heather was awarded "Provost" Scholar prior to the stroke in December and is so driven and determined to do well.

She is frustrated, angry and struggles with anxiety. None of which I feel is uncalled for. Yet I pray for direction and wisdom on how to help my baby. As a dad I just want to fix it. Unfortunately, this not an option. In my heart, I believe that GOD does have this and for his glory. We all need to be patient and let him do his work.

Please also pray for Lynn. This has been extremely hard on her. She did not leave Heather in the hospital for four days and slept in a chair beside her bed. She too is struggling with anger and frustration.

Lauren has done so many wonderful acts of kindness to help us all. She is an amazing sister and truly loves Heather and our family.

Thank you all for your continued thoughts and prayers. They are so very much appreciated.

Randy.

Heather Update – November 26, 2012

Friends,

Yesterday Heather went back to the Presbyterian hospital due to her not feeling well, weakness in her left extremities and very severe headache. They did another cat scan and the good news was that there was no sign of any new bleed. She was heading back to school when it just got unbearable. So, she called Lynn and I and we met her and Greg at the emergency room. They did release her last night and she stayed home until late this morning.

As we continue to ask for prayers for complete healing and recovery, we are also asking for GOD to give her peace. She is fighting the fear and anxiety brought on after this last bleed. She is so very strong in her faith and determination. Yet, struggles with questions and frustrations brought on by her situation.

She is back at IUP tonight and tomorrow Lynn and I are going there to meet with her academic advisor and two of her professors to discuss any and all options to complete this semester. She has worked so very hard to maintain her high academic standards even though she could have just given up at any time and it would have been understandable.

Now with only three weeks remaining in the semester we are hoping and praying that they will be supportive in her efforts to complete the semester and help her in developing a plan which will allow her to graduate in the near future.

I cannot express how thankful we are for your continued prayers and encouragement.

Randy.

Heather Update – November 28, 2012

Friends,

Went to IUP yesterday and spent most of the day meeting with the Assistant Dean, Advisor, Heather's professors and the landlord.

Overall, that was very productive and promising. They were all very sympathetic to her situation. I am very glad I went and could feel like I was able to do something for my daughter.

As I mentioned in an earlier message, we are trying to get her through this semester with only a couple of weeks remaining. The Dean and faculty are working on some options for Heather so she may be able to maintain her academic achievements from this semester. We were able to develop a very light schedule moving forward over the spring and summer semesters so that she will be able to graduate next year.

She was required to take on a year lease for her apartment and they believe they can find someone else for that 2nd half of the year. We are praying that they will terminate the lease this calendar year, so we do not even have to think about that burden and expense.

Unfortunately, after our last meeting Heather's stroke like

symptoms intensified and we rushed her to the hospital in Pittsburgh. She was admitted last night and is going through more tests to try to help her. After another Cat scans and MRI, they have determined that there were no further bleeds (Thank you, Jesus). Today they are running blood tests to see if there is something else causing these symptoms. We are hoping that they have just not hit the right combination of steroids and pain medicines for her to recover. We remain confident that she is in very good hands and will find a solution. A high definition MRI is scheduled for 7:30AM tomorrow as a complete picture of the situation.

Please continue to pray for Heather. For complete healing, peace of mind and continued strength and faith that GOD has her and will not let go.

Heather Update – December 1, 2012

Friends,

Heather's symptoms have dramatically increased and it has been determined that she has experienced another bleed. Due to this event she must have surgery, which is scheduled for next Tuesday assuming she does not worsen before. The objective is to remove the cavernous malformation. Obviously, this is a very serious surgery, especially with where it is located on her thalamus.

We believe in the neurological team. They have explained the benefits and the consequences to Heather and she is in agreement that this is necessary. She is the strongest young women that I have ever met. She is scared yet her faith is unshakable. She told me tonight that she and Greg have been praying for GOD to give them a very clear direction on next steps. As she told me tonight, even though she is sad and scared it could not be more clear on what she needs to do. She needs prayers. Prayers to guide the doctors and staff. Prayers for peace as she waits for the operation. Prayers for no long term negative physical or mental effects. Prayers for speedy and total recovery.

Thank you very much.
Randy.

109

Heather Update – December 3, 2012

Friends,

On Friday afternoon Heather experienced a major setback with another bleed. She was transferred to ICU and we have lived here ever since. It has been very touch and go as far as her condition, controlling the pain and developing a plan for next steps. At this moment she is having another MRI to map the surgical path for her surgery scheduled for tomorrow. At this point the doctors are saying that after surgery, she will continue to be monitored in ICU for 3 to 5 days. Then if things go as planned, she will be transferred to Mercy Hospital for what could be a month-long rehab or longer.

Keep the prayers coming for a flawless procedure and speedy and complete recovery. We are doing the best we can and trying to keep Heather lifted up. She is the most courageous person I have ever known.

One thing I have asked everyone is if anyone knows any Senior Administrators at IUP, with this new set back of Heather having to undergo surgery, we do not believe that an offer of "Incomplete" is going to work since her recovery and abilities will be unknown possibly for a very long time. What we are trying to do is get her professors to judge Heather's work based on her performance all semester. This is just another stressor for her and in my opinion totally unnecessary. She has worked so very hard and is so close to graduation that not passing any of these classes would be just another blow to someone that has been so dedicated to her education for years and now with two weeks remaining will be penalized for something totally out of her control.

Please pray for my baby with all of your heart and ask GOD for Heather to have that fighting chance, so that she may honor and glorify a miraculous recovery. Pastor Scott used an analogy last evening that was perfect. He told us about his boxing days and how the worst time was waiting in the locker room. Where so many thoughts run through your mind when you just want to get into the ring hear the bell and give it your best. We are in the locker room today and are praying for Heather to knock out this cavernous malformation cold tomorrow. So she may get on with her life as the true champion that she is.

Thank you very much,

Randy.

Heather Update – December 4, 2012

Friends,

Praise the Lord. Thank you, Jesus. We just got word that Heather got out of surgery. They say "it went very well and believe they got the cavernous malformation out, " she does have significant left sided weaknesses. They also informed us that they were able to remove her breathing tube already as Lynn was on the phone with Dr. Friedlander, she said WOW (which I took as a positive medical term). She is back in ICU and will remain there for 3 to 5 days. If all goes well with the post-surgery, she will be moved to a step-down ward here at Presbyterian in 3 to 5 days. Then the plan is to move to Mercy Hospital for OT & PT for probably a month. Then continued rehab based on needs as time will tell.

The doctors informed us that her situation had become life threatening this week. So, it is with great relief and appreciation she will now be able to begin this long journey to recovery. Please continue to pray for a speedy recovery, complete cognitive and physical abilities. She is a fighter and told us she was "ready" last night and again this morning before the surgery. She just wanted that thing out of her head and not have to worry everyday like she has over the last year of whether this thing was going to bleed again and what damage it was going to do. Not to mention the issues of not feeling well and other related symptoms.

Since we are far from truly knowing the effects of this complex surgery, we are so appreciative that she is with us and now has the opportunity to begin again.

Please continue your prayers and from my heart I cannot tell you how much my family and I appreciate all of you. I will continue to keep you updated.

Randy.

Heather Update – December 5, 2012

Friends,

Thank you for your continued prayers and keep them coming. Last night when the nurses kicked Lynn and I out of the room Heather was unable to move anything on her left side. This morning around 7AM a doctor came in to check and she was able to slightly move her toes and her fingers on her left side. You would have thought Lynn and I had just won the biggest lottery ever. This evening Dr. Friedlander came in and she was able to grasp his finger, and move her leg slightly. Lynn asked if he thought she was doing well? His response, "she is not doing well, she is doing Phenomenal". He ordered the drain from her brain removed this evening, that appears to have gone well as well.

There are no real words that can express our gratitude for these many blessings of which we are sure have been given due to all of your prayers and the 1,000's of others around the world that have been praying for Heather. We know this is just the beginning, but we are so very thankful for this opportunity. Heather is going to do something "Phenomenal" with her life and it is only because of the Grace of GOD.

Randy.

Heather Update – December 6, 2012

Friends,

It has been quite a day. Heather has made additional positive movements in left hand, foot and leg. Reminds us of the excitement when she took her first steps as a baby, probably better this time because we were not sure we would see that again. Bandages are off, exposing her shaved scalp, the incision area from top of her forehead curving down behind her right ear. They gave her a sponge bath, washed her hair and she looks beautiful. They have removed the catheter and one iv. They have left a monitor in her scull which monitors the pressure inside. We are told that is next to come out.

The exciting news is they have released her from ICU and moved her to a step-down unit. They had originally estimated 3 to 5 days in post-op ICU yet here we sit less than 2 days out. We are being told that all is looking good, yet Heather is fighting extreme headaches. When asked about the pain level on a scale of 1 to 10 she may say 13. We are confident that they will come up with the right combination of medicines to help her. Even while experiencing this excruciating pain Heather continues to be pleasant and polite.

Please continue to pray for Heather's continued recovery and that they can get control of the pain. She is concerned about the removal of the monitor because it is very deep in her brain.

I sit here in awe of GOD's blessings and glory. With a new appreciation for life and the simplest of pleasures. Thankful for the faith that continues to get us through this very difficult time and for the gifts GOD has given these very smart and talented medical professionals. For your continued prayers and support which always seems to lift us up at our lowest moments.

Thank you all,

Randy Abramovic.

Heather Update – December 7, 2012

Friends,

This morning they removed the brain pressure monitor which caused her great pain. Pain seems to be the current mountain to climb. They are getting better with the combinations of medications to help her and she has gone from a 13 to an 8 to a 4 at one point today on a pain scale from 1 to 10. They have explained that this is very typical with major surgery like she has experienced. The good thing is that all these devices have now been removed and can let the healing begin.

Another positive step forward for Heather today. Literally the physical therapists had her standing and with their physical assistance were able to take 5 steps forward. Dr. Friedlander just left and said he was "amazed" at her progress. He has ordered another fiber tracking MRI for Monday morning. If all goes well with that, she will be transferred to Mercy Hospital for in-patient physical and occupational therapy.

A technical source we have met has shared their professional opinion of her MRI's. This person told us that Heather's scan on Monday prior to her operation showed her in an urgent and critical situation. Post operation scans, "amazing, actually look like a new brain".

That makes two different people today in totally different times and situations that have used the word "amazed" or "amazing" to describe Heather's situation or progress. We think that it is GOD that is amazing! He continues to hear all our prayers and is blessing Heather with recovery.

Please keep those prayers coming for her continued recovery and her "amazing" outlook.

Thank you and may GOD bless all of you for helping lift Heather up.

Randy Abramovic.

Heather Update – December 10, 2012

Friends,

It is very hard to believe that it has been two weeks since we rushed Heather to the hospital. She has endured more during this time than most people do in their lifetime. She continues to "Amaze" everyone with her courage and positive attitude while fighting the pain that is off the charts. She had another fiber mapping MRI today of which we have not received any information, but they have transferred her from Presbyterian Hospital to Mercy Hospital where she will begin her long road to physical and occupational therapy beginning tomorrow.

She is scared. We are asking for prayers to comfort Heather in this next stage of recovery. To give her strength to persevere and maintain her confidence and determination. There is no doubt this will be very hard for her yet we know she will do her very best she can. We also ask for prayers for TOTAL RECOVERY. That she may take this awful experience and find ways to help others in the future and glorify GOD with her testimony.

Please also pray for Lynn, who has not left Heather for the last 14 days. She is an amazing selfless, loving mother. As I write this note, I will be taking her home tonight where I hope she can get some rest and sleep in a bed for the first time since this began.

Thank you all again for your prayers and support. There is no doubt that these prayers have carried us to be able to be strong for Heather and each other.

Randy Abramovic.

Heather Update – December 13, 2012

Friends,

Heather began her physical and occupational therapy on Tuesday which was a week after her brain surgery. She continues to "Amaze" us all with her determination and faith. Though she now wears a 15" incision from her right temple in the center of her forehead, the twinkle in her eyes is back. We are so pleased with the staff, facilities and overall atmosphere at Mercy Hospital.

No one can tell us what functions Heather will regain at this point and she continues to struggle with pain levels in the 7 - 9 range vs. The 9 - 13 range a few days ago. There is no doubt that GOD has blessed Heater and our family. She is alive getting better every day and that is a huge blessing some may say a miracle (I do). She has a long road ahead for recovery and will face it a day at a time.

We cannot thank you all enough for your continued prayers. There is no doubt that your prayers are being answered and expanded through your efforts to share these prayer requests with others, please continue and pray for Heather's TOTAL RECOVERY.

Randy Abramovic.

Heather Update – December 15, 2012

Friends,

Heather has been informed that she will remain at Mercy Hospital for rehab until December 31. Needless to say, spending Christmas is not exactly where she was hoping to be. She continues to amaze me at her strength and determination to give 100% of mind and body to regain her basic functions.

Today she asked me to be with her during her two therapy sessions. She talked to me about how hard and frustrating it is to ask for something to move and it takes such willpower and determination to move it at all. While fighting a headache at the 10 level. Then how exhausted she is afterwards. I reminded her of one week ago when she was unable to move anything on her left side and how impressive her progress is.

Though this breaks my heart to see her struggle like this. Her strength and determination are "AMAZING". It is her true character of faith, hope and love that beams from her expressions and statements.

Please continue to pray for Heather's "Total Recovery" and to maintain her strength and determination during this very difficult time.

Randy Abramovic.

Heather Update – December 23, 2012

Friends,

Below is a post from Face Book that Heather wrote on Friday to give her perspective of her situation.

Heather wrote: "Exactly one year ago today I started the darkest time of my life, it has been such a hard and tiring year, 5 brain hemorrhages, gamma knife surgery, and a craniotomy. Praying for a break, but a lot of good things have come out of this, so I'm thankful, but want to start living my life again. I couldn't have survived this year without my fiancé and family and God holding my hand each step of the way."

It has only been a little over three weeks since Heather's brain surgery and being paralyzed on the left side post-surgery. She has been at Mercy Hospital since December 10th with daily rehabilitation. She is working so hard. To watch her determination in her eyes and expressions is daunting. Yesterday she had some amazing breakthroughs. First, she walked with a leg brace on her left leg unassisted down a long hall and back! The other is that she hit a new pain level low of 3. You may remember that only a few weeks ago, she was at a 13 out of 10.

Please continue to pray for Heather's COMPLETE RECOVERY. She has a long road ahead. GOD has blessed her with life, an amazing faith during this dark time and an appreciation for everything she has. She continues to amaze all in her steps of recovery and her positive outlook. She exudes the Christmas Spirit of giving. Giving 100% of herself to reach her GOD given potential and showing sincere appreciation for all of you that have helped and prayed for her.

Merry Christmas to all of you and may GOD bless you and your families.
Randy Abramovic.

Heather Update – December 28, 2012

Friends,

We were able to get a twelve-hour pass for Heather to go home for Christmas. She said, " it was wonderful, best Christmas ever". It was the first time outside a hospital in over a month.

The doctors have extended her rehabilitation for a few additional days. She is now scheduled to be released from Mercy Hospital on January 3rd. The extension is to enable her to continue her very regimented rehabilitation as long as possible. She is then scheduled for outpatient rehabilitation at Health South in Harmarville Health South.

She continues to amaze us all. She is working so very hard and is determined to continue to improve every day. Today she walked further than she has since she got here with a leg brace and cane. Her headaches have been kept in check with new medicines and basically, she is at a "0" there. Unfortunately, she continues to have pain in her jaw post-surgery, which they believe was caused during surgery "TMJ". Our hope is to get her to a specialist on that once she is released.

Please continue to pray for Heather's "Complete Recovery". Pleased as she is with her continued improvements with her left leg. Her left arm and hand are frustrating her. She tells us that she focuses and commands fingers, wrist and arm to move with very little response if any at this point. We have been told that this is usually a much longer recovery and that she needs to continue to work on it and be patient. Her response has been, a cute little smile and determination in her eyes of, I'll show you."

While she continues to amaze all in her cognitive and physical abilities in such a short period of time. The most amazing thing is her attitude and appreciation for all the support, love and prayers she receives.

Yesterday Greg (Finance") and three very special people from our church moved Heather's things from her apartment to our home. On November 27th I had given the apartment management notice in person of her situation and the need to terminate her lease for the spring semester. I have kept them apprised of her situation and that there is absolutely no chance of her return in the spring. At this point I have been unable to get a response from the apartment owners. The reason I am sharing this situation with you is to ask for prayers to soften the apartment owners' hearts to be compassionate due to these very unfortunate circumstances. To take the burden off Heather so that she may be able to focus on her recovery. The apartment complex is Philadelphia Square Apartments in Indiana PA. If anyone knows the owners or has any other suggestions, they would be greatly appreciated.

Thank you again for your loving prayers they have made all the difference to Heather and our family.

Randy Abramovic.

Heather Update – January 6, 2013

Friends,

Heather completed her In Patient therapy at Mercy Hospital on Thursday as planned. She is now home and continues to amaze all that have seen her progress. The absolute miracle is that at this point her short- and long-term memory as well as personality and cognitive skills appear to be unaffected by her brain surgery. It is an absolute blessing and we could not be more thankful to GOD for giving her this gift,

Heather's attitude is "the harder I work now will result in my greatest recovery physically". She continues to be diligent about doing her exercises that the OT and PT therapists showed her at Mercy Hospital. We continue to observe her left leg getting stronger and today she actually lifted it up from a sitting position. She had been using her right leg to lift and move it. Needless to say, there were many shouts of joy and appreciation for another small yet very positive step forward.

Lack of movement in her left arm and hand continue to frustrate her. She has full faith that these functions will return and she needs to be patient. As she talks about her resolve to recover completely, I can only feel such a sense of pride in my daughter. It is with great sadness that I watch her struggle with her current dependence, yet it has brought our family closer together, opened our eyes to appreciate all of our blessings and strengthened our faith in Jesus Christ which is the most important thing.

On Wednesday she will begin her outpatient therapy at Health South Rehabilitation Center. Please continue to pray for her complete recovery, continued strength and faith that she will surely need over her long journey ahead.

We cannot thank you enough for your prayers, visits and many acts of kindness. They are all greatly appreciated during this very difficult time.

Randy Abramovic.

Heather Update – January 16, 2013

Friends,

Praise the LORD!!! I cannot imagine a more fitting description of the news today.

On Monday, Heather had a follow up MRI with the fiber tracking at Presbyterian Hospital. Today we met with Dr. Friedlander and his associates. After checking Heather's physical abilities for strength and movement, he asked her when her surgery was. She told him 6 weeks ago yesterday. "WOW, you are doing amazing", was his response. He then took us to a special viewing office to review the results of Monday's MRI. They showed us the graphic images of the scans and explained the differences of before and after surgery. Everything looks very promising for continued improvement and recovery.

We also discovered some very interesting facts that can only be attributed to GOD's Divine Intervention.

- We were reaching out to neurosurgeons around the country. We thought that one we had met with in Chicago a couple of times was the right one because of his experience with cavernous malformations, yet he recommended Dr. Friedlander in Pittsburgh should the need for surgery arise.

- We were praying for the lesion not to bleed again. Miraculously due to it bleeding (5 X) it pushed the cavernous malformation to an area which allowed it to be removed.

- We also learned today that Presbyterian Hospital in Pittsburgh is the only hospital in the "**World**" currently using the MRI fiber tracking for this type of brain surgery. The doctor explained how this allowed them to see and map out every detail of the surgery and not cause any major damage. "It allowed us to see".

- Dr. Friedlander asked if Heather could come to his office because he had another patient that 2.5 years ago underwent very similar surgery and she was in for a follow up visit from Baltimore, MD. This young woman has regained her independence and the majority of her physical and cognitive abilities. He informed them both that he wanted them to meet because, they both have extremely positive outlooks and the drive and determination to "beat their situation and not let the situation beat them". They both shared battle scars, pain stories and email addresses.

Heather is now in outpatient rehabilitation and has a long road ahead for recovery. Please continue to pray for her complete recovery and ability to remain positive and focused.

We know GOD has heard all your prayers. He has blessed Heather with life, hope for the future and surrounding her with people who love her.

Randy Abramovic.

Heather Update – February 6, 2013

Friends,

The last couple of weeks was an assortment of up and downs for Heather. She continues to work extremely hard at Health South in her Occupational & Physical Therapy. Her determination is evident in everything she is asked to do. Yet she talks about how frustrating it is to will a part of her body to function and nothing happens or she cannot do the simplest of things like turning a doorknob or opening anything due to the very limited movement in her left hand and arm. Requiring assistance to put her leg brace on so she can walk. Heather makes great improvements every day and is fully aware of her challenges and the time that it is going to take to get as much function back as possible. It may require years of continued therapy and special equipment to give her the greatest opportunity to recover.

As you may be aware Heather is engaged to be married. Last weekend we went to Saint Paul's Cathedral, where she and Greg would like to have their ceremony in 2014. She walked up several steps surrounded by three of us to help and assure she did not fall. She and Greg walked down the center isle and went to the alter. We prayed that the next time she made this journey it would be walking unassisted, by my side to give her away and she would be able to throw her bouquet with her left hand. All indications show with uninterrupted and dedicated efforts she may well get her prayers answered.

She is committed to her recovery, but has hit a stumbling block. Her insurance is running out for her much-needed outpatient physical and occupational therapy.

We have started to explore ways to ensure that she continues to get the help she needs so desperately. Currently Heather is doing 3 days a week at an estimated cost of $900.00 per week. My eldest daughter Lauren has coordinated a distributor to host a Premier Jewelry Party at our home on February 24th with 50% of profits going to her outpatient therapy. We are also setting up an account that will accept donations which will go directly to Heather's therapy expenses.

Donations can be sent to:

"Heather's Fight for Therapy Fund"

3097 Henrich Farm Lane

Allison Park, PA 15101

Contact Lynn, about the Jewelry Party 412.xxx-xxxx

Please continue to pray for Heather's complete and total recovery and that we may overcome this mountain. We believe that GOD has performed a miracle with her survival and amazing recovery. We cannot express fully our appreciation for your continued support. Your thoughts, prayers and acts of kindness are what is giving us hope and strength to carry on.

Thank you,

Randy Abramovic.

Heather Update – February 25, 2013

Friends,

Heather continues to fight for recovery. Her attitude is remarkable and her faith unshakable. Unfortunately, her insurance coverage for her days of therapy has expired.

Heather told a man at church yesterday who stopped her and asked what had happened as she walked with her brace and cane through the lobby. She shared her story of this enormous life trial and then she said, "I don't know what GOD wants me to do with this at this point, but I am absolutely sure he is going to have me do great things to help others".

Attached is: Heather's Story: Living Life with Faith Not Fear I believe that this will give you a better perspective of where she was and how far she has to go.

In my last update I asked for prayers and donations. We cannot thank you enough for those donations and for your continued prayers. Please continue to pray for Heather. Prayers of sustained hope for her future, clear direction how GOD would like her to use this devastating trail for good. For the resources to continue her therapy so she may experience complete recovery and her independence.

Thank you and may GOD bless you,

Randy Abramovic.

Heather's "Thank you note" to me – February 26, 2013

I cannot thank you enough for your support and generosity through my long road to recovery. I am so appreciative and grateful for your kindness. "I can do all things through Christ who strengthens me." Philippians. 4:13.

Thank you, Dad,

Heather Abramovic.

Heather Update – March 15, 2013

Friends,

What a wonderful week it has been. Heather has made some major steps forward, and I mean that literally. On Wednesday she underwent Targeted Botox Injections in both her arm and leg. She said it was painful, but compared to having brain surgery it was nothing. As you can see, she has still got her sense of humor. The whole idea is for the Botox to weaken the large muscles in her arm and leg so that her smaller muscles have a better chance of reconnecting with her brain signals. We will know in about three weeks if the treatment is working.

On Sunday she said, "Dad, I want to give you a hug", which is very common around our house, so I didn't give it much thought until I felt her left arm touching my back. It has only been three months since her brain surgery and at that point she was paralyzed on her left side. This is one of those moments like watching a baby take its first step. It was a small movement, but we'll take it. She got her Saebo Flex which is a custom fabricated wrist, hand and finger orthoses so that she is now able to do some OT at home every day.

Today I went to therapy with her and they fitted her with a device called a Bioness which sends an electronic signal to her leg above her brace. The hope being it would allow her to smooth out her gait. She walked up and down two flights of steps and a cumulative distance of one mile, by the time her therapy session was over. At the end they actually turned off the stimulation and she was still able to walk briskly and normally. Her PT therapist was stunned. He had mentioned he thought it might help, but never imagined her magnificent success. What a blessing. Heather said she had not felt so good about herself in over three months and this gave her even more motivation to keep working hard.

We received the proceeds from the two fundraisers that were put on for "Heather's Fight For Therapy Fund" and your generous donations. For those of you that participated and have donated we cannot thank you enough. It has allowed her to continue therapy uninterrupted which is so critical as her brain is trying to reconnect and function. We are planning another fundraiser in June and will keep you posted on that.

She has a long road ahead. Only GOD knows what her needs are going to be. So, I ask that you all continue to pray for her 100% recovery. In addition, prayers for a clear life vision. One that will allow her to share her story and glorify GOD for the miracle of life and the blessings he has given her in this journey.

Thank you all again. It is impossible to express our true gratitude through this very difficult time.

Randy Abramovic.

Heather Update – April 3, 2013

Friends,

Today was a very exciting and encouraging day for Heather. Last week she had two MRIs the regular and the fiber tracking as a scheduled follow up from her surgery. Today we met with Dr. Friedlander, a neurosurgeon and Dr Galang, who did the Botox treatments three weeks ago. Both were so very pleased with her recovery to date. It will be four months tomorrow since her brain surgery. The MRIs show the brain healing and no sign of the cavernous angioma.

Heather is working so very hard in therapy and exercises at home. She continues her determination to recover fully. She said this weekend that she feels that she has regained about 70% of her strength in her left leg. She is now able to walk short distances with her leg brace, but without the assistance of her cane. She can close her fingers on her left hand but is unable to open them at this point and has very limited movement in her left arm. Both doctors could not have been more encouraging and feel that with her continued therapy and determination she will continue to improve.

125

We could not feel more blessed than we do today. Four months ago, we may have lost our daughter. Today she has the twinkle back in her eyes and that very special smile. She is so thankful to GOD for saving her life and has opened her eyes to appreciate every little moment and ability. She tells us she is praying for direction on how she can take this unfortunate experience and use it to help others.

We know our prayers are being answered. This is nothing short of a miracle. GOD has a wonderful plan for Heather's life and she is going to do amazing things with it. We do ask that you continue to pray for her total recovery, the strength to persevere and her emotional well-being as she continues to eliminate her medications. She has a long road ahead but we know that as a family, we can endure and with all of your support and prayers which has been so greatly appreciated, we will get through this together.

With all sincerity,

Randy Abramovic.

Heather Update – April 23, 2013

Friends,

Yesterday, we met with Dr. Friedlander and the neurosurgery team. The update was nothing short of a miracle. We reviewed Heather's most recent HD Fiber Tracking MRI, video clip of her brain surgery and colorful fiber tracking scans over the last year as a comparison of the connections from the brain to the extremities. It shows the fibers intact and beginning to react again. Dr. Friedlander explained how this new fiber tracking technology allowed him to get to the lesion and remove it while avoiding damaging other vital nerve fibers. While Heather was in ICU, experiencing her fifth brain hemorrhage that paralyzed her left side, they knew surgery was their only option. In the past, they would have cut across and removed the lesion leaving her paralyzed on her left side, if not worst. They may have saved her life, contributed the damage done by the hemorrhage as a permanent outcome. Yet, due to today's talent and technology (God's Handy Work / Spiritual Gifts) they were able to reach the cavernous malformation in the center of her brain without damaging those nerve fibers and giving her this opportunity to heal and recover.

There was no shortage of hugs, clapping and thankful praises and a few tears of happiness and relief. Our daughter is blessed with a new hopeful beginning.

As wonderful and encouraging as yesterday's news was for Heather, she shared with me her concerns and frustrations. She lives with a constant reminder of her current disability. Her very limited ability to move her left arm, hand or unclench her fingers. She explains how frustrating it is to be dependent and restricted physically. How she misses doing the most common of tasks. She realizes that she needs to be patient and continue to work as hard as possible to recover fully. Heather recognizes her many blessings and is grateful for her life and her recovery to this point. She knows that GOD has spared her for a great reason and expects her to use this for good.

Please continue to pray for Heather. For her complete and total recovery and the strength and courage to persevere along this long road to recovery. To show her clearly how God wants to use this in her life for the benefit of others and his glory.

We cannot thank you enough for your generous support and prayers that have carried us though this very difficult period in our lives.

Sincerely,

Randy Abramovic.

Heather Update – June 8, 2013

Friends,

Very tough week for Heather, on Monday the insurance company denied the prescribed Botox treatments which allow for her larger muscles to relax and not hinder her recovery in her left arm, hand and leg. We were told it would be out of pocket expense at $4,000.00 per treatment. So, we cried together and prayed together. On Thursday we actually took Heather along to our weekly couples' bible study and we prayed for her together.

Friday in therapy she was very frustrated because of the tone (muscle contraction) that physically clenches her fingers and contracts her arm upward. She is working so very hard to regain her mobility and this prevents her smaller muscles from reacting to the therapy. In the true Heather style, she still found the strength to go and meet with another person who is afflicted with several cavernous malformations on her brain, but is not as fortunate to have the family and friends support like Heather.

Friday afternoon we got a phone message from Mercy Hospital that the insurance company has reconsidered and has approved the Botox treatments every three months for a whole year. Praise GOD!!! We could not feel more blessed than we do. This is a huge weight lifted up. We give complete credit to all of your prayers. Please continue praying for Heather's complete recovery. You will be a part of something very special that she is going to do with all of this suffering and turn it into something very good for others. Another example of her true spirit is that she asked if we would take her to Homewood last night so we could serve food to less fortunate people. We did and it was a wonderful experience, the level of appreciation for a hot meal and a cookie was very humbling.

Her Botox treatments are scheduled for June 19th and we ask for prayers that they are effective.

Thank you all again for your generosity and prayers. Heather would not be recovering as well as she is without them.

Randy Abramovic

P.S. If you have not seen her web site yet here is a hot link to her story, video and ability to register for the upcoming event "Enjoy The Moment" http://HeathersFight.com

Heather Update – July 5, 2013

Friends,

July 4th marked the 7th month since Heather's miraculous brain surgery that saved her life. God has blessed her with substantial recovery to date. She continues to work so very hard at her therapy and dealing with her current physical limitations of which we hope and pray she will overcome with prayers, time and therapy.

Her fundraiser last week was nothing short of amazing. The venue was filled with positive energy, love and the Holy Spirit. Sally Wiggin (WTAE News anchor) shared stories of how she first met Heather when she was 4 years old and how she has watched her grow and develop into such a special woman. Andy Russell (Former Pittsburgh Steeler, 2-time super bowl champion) shared his thoughts and comparisons to Heather's fight and playing professional football as part of the "Steel Curtain". Dr Robert Friedlander (Chairman of Neurological Surgery UPMC & Surgeon that saved her life) shared Heather's experience from a neurosurgeon's perspective supported by Heather's brain scans over the last 18 months and a video clip of the actual removal of the cavernous malformation. Heather spoke about her perspective and the three things she has learned from her suffering. One, GOD pulled her through surgery for a purpose which she will pursue helping others the rest of her life, Two, GOD continues to heal her which she is so very grateful for her progress and hope of complete recovery, Third, GOD has given her a supportive, loving family and Greg her fiancé'. I spoke and shared my Divine vision at her bedside right after surgery. As clear as could be GOD showed me her walking down the aisle at her sister Lauren's wedding (She did May 25), second, she showed me Heather walking down the aisle at her wedding and lastly, he showed me a vision of her in a hospital bed. Yet this time it was for a wonderful blessing of life. She was ready to give birth. Then, as clear as could be he told me to tell her, "Heather, go have a wonderful life". I grabbed a napkin off a table in ICU and wrote that note to her from GOD and shared that with everyone.

Attached is a song which was written and sung by Kaleb Jones from Nashville a nationally recognized voice, songwriter and friend of Heather's.

https://soundcloud.com/user117607031/do-not-be-afraid

Heather ended with this statement that holds true for all of you that have so generously supported her and continue to pray for her complete recovery.

"I cannot THANK YOU enough for your support and generosity through my long road to recovery. I am so appreciative and grateful for your kindness."

Heather Abramovic.

Heather Update – August 4, 2013

Friends,

Today is 8 months since Heather's brain surgery. Much has happened that I would like to share with you all. She continues to work so very hard at therapy, both in Harmarville Rehabilitation and at home. This past Friday she was cleared to walk without her AFO (Leg & Ankle Brace). It was a wonderful thing to see it laying on the floor and her walk without it. Though her gait is not very smooth she is very pleased to be released from it. She is still unable to move her left hand, fingers and arm. This is a huge frustration for her. Her therapists have begun a new therapy called "Interactive Metronome" (IM). IM neurological and motor rehabilitation is an advanced brain-based therapy designed to promote and enhance brain performance and recovery. This is accomplished by using innovative neurosensory and neuromotor exercises developed to improve the brain's inherent ability to repair or remodel itself through a process called neuroplasticity.

Heather completed a class online toward her graduation. Earned an "A" and is back on track to complete her requirements for graduation next Spring. She is so determined not to let anything get in her way and maintain her high academic standards. She is a true inspiration.

This is something I read recently and has become kind of a mantra for my family and I that I wanted to share with you. I believe it to be very appropriate no matter what our circumstances are.

Romans 12:12

"Be glad for all God is planning for you. Be patient in trouble, and always be prayerful."

Please continue to pray for Heather's complete and total recovery.

Sincerely,

Randy Abramovic.

Heather Update – August 29, 2013

Friends,

My intent was to send an update on September 4th which will mark 9 months since Heather's brain surgery, but I need to send a praise report to the world. Heather just called me after leaving therapy today and she said she had great news. "DAD, I moved my left hand and fingers unassisted 4 times in therapy." She has been unable to do this in 9 months.

As I sit here with tears of absolute joy, I wanted to share this miracle with you. She still has so far to go, but to me this shows that GOD is healing her and gives her hope.

Please continue to pray for Heather's complete and total recovery.

Randy Abramovic.

Heather Update – September 22, 2013

Friends,

As we approach the 10-month mark since Heather's brain surgery (November 4th) I wanted to share these thoughts and updates. She continues to struggle with functional abilities to move her left arm and hand to perform daily tasks. She has had moments which we see as great hope and blessings. Heather's left leg has improved and she hopes with time and therapy to get back to a point where she can run again. Next Friday Heather will be fitted with an electrical stimulation device for her hand called a Bioness. We have committed to renting it for three months with the option to buy if it works. The device sends electrical impulses to stimulate muscles to open and close her fingers.

This past Friday Heather was recognized at the "2013 HealthSouth Harmarville Rex Newton, MD Rehab Champions Awards Luncheon". She was awarded "Outpatient Rehab Champion" presented by both her OT and PT therapist. It was a beautiful affair and an honor to hear about Heather's progress, tenacity and her encouragement to others.

Heather has also been asked to be part of a UPMC TV commercial which will be filmed in late October or early November.

God has given her the strength to persevere. To glorify him for her continued progress and to encourage others that she comes into contact with.

Please continue to pray for her complete and total recovery. That her spirit may shine brighter and touch more hearts over time and that she is blessed with the inner strength for her long journey ahead.

My sincere thanks to all of you,

Randy Abramovic.

Heather Update – October 5, 2013

Friends,

Yesterday marked the 10th month since Heather's brain surgery. It is an amazing blessing of how far she has come. Her faith and tenacity to persevere is nothing short of a miracle. She could have given up at any time and just said she has had enough. Yet, she continues to set new goals for herself and works toward them. She has her days that she is sad and frustrated with her current physical limitations. But she always finds the strength and peace to continue. There is no doubt in my mind that she has been blessed with the opportunity to use her suffering to bless others and share how faith in Jesus Christ is the only way.

Over the past week she has been fitted with the electrical stimulation device (Bioness) and has moved her little and index finger in therapy again unassisted. On Wednesday she had her 10-month post op MRI and Dr. Friedlander told her how good and clear everything is looking. Thank you, Jesus. Dr. Friedlander also told her that she would not need another scheduled MRI for one year. This is exactly the kind of encouragement she needed.

Last Sunday we all participated in the Pittsburgh Great Race. Lynn, Greg, Heather and I walked the 5K together. While Lauren and Bob ran 5K and 10K respectively. It was a beautiful morning and Heather talked about how meaningful it was for her to be able to walk that far in 1 hour 6 minutes. What was really ironic is that it started in front of Presbyterian Hospital where she had her surgery and we walked past Mercy Hospital where she spent a month in inpatient rehabilitation. Heather said it was a wonderful event, though very draining both physically and emotionally. Which has led her to set a new goal of running the 5K next year.

Please continue to keep Heather in your prayers for complete and total recovery. That GOD will give her clear directions for her path in life, be patient in her suffering and always be prayerful and thankful for her many blessings.

Hope this note finds you and your family well. We are so appreciative of all of your prayers and support.

My sincere thanks to all of you.

Randy Abramovic.

Heather Update – November 5, 2013

Friends,

November 4th marked 11 months since Heather's brain surgery. When we brought her home 9 months ago, she was totally dependent on us and in a wheel chair. In our eyes she has made huge improvements and she has. Yet, her inability to move her left arm, hand and fingers are a tremendous burden and frustration to her as I can only imagine. She is continuing her therapy at Harmarville and works with the electrical stimulation device (Bioness) daily. The technology is amazing and a blessing. To watch her open her fingers and move her wrist with the electrical assistance is encouraging.

Last week UPMC's marketing department shot a TV commercial at our barn where we keep Darius our horse and in our home. It was an all-day affair from 6AM to 4:30PM with 50 people involved in the production. It is quite an honor that they think this highly of Heather, her attitude and her progress. She glowed. You would have thought she did this every day. It will be very exciting to see her on the air.

Please pray for Heather. That somehow God reveals his purpose for her suffering, for total recovery and peace while she waits patiently.

Thank you all for your continued prayers and support. It is so greatly appreciated and helping.

My sincere thanks to all of you.

Randy Abramovic.

Heather Update – November 24, 2013

Friends,

As we approach the 1year mark since Heather's brain surgery, I wanted to update you and share a moment from yesterday that illustrates Heather's determination and courage. On Friday at physical therapy she asked if she could run? Her PT, Josh agreed to try only if she wore her leg brace and he sidestepped beside her. Well, she did it for a short distance. Though she told me it requires her total mental focus and physically is exhausting it felt wonderful. Only 10 months ago we brought her home in a wheelchair and totally dependent for everything. Yesterday she asked if I would take her to Hampton High School track to see her run. In 28-degree weather and snow flurries we went to the track and I could not contain myself from pulling out my iPhone and recording this short video.

God has blessed Heather with a wonderful spirit and strength. A love for life and others that is unmistakable.

Please continue to pray for her total and complete recovery. As we approach this anniversary, she has begun to experience some double vision. She had another MRI on November 14th and everything continues to look clear. We are being told that this does happen and they are working on a plan to treat it with corrective lens. Heather continues to work daily with the Bioness (electrical stimulation deice) to gain function back in her left arm, hand and fingers.

During this season of giving thanks. I want to extend our sincere thanks to all of you. We could not have gotten through this without your prayers and support. God has taught us so many things. To always lean on him, not to take anything for granted and love each other.

May God bless you and your families.

Randy Abramovic.

Heather Update – December 25, 2013

Friends,

I cannot think of a more appropriate day than Christmas Day to reflect on the past year and Heather's progress. Last Christmas she was at Mercy Hospital for inpatient therapy and they granted her a six-hour pass to go home. At that time, she was on over 10 prescription medicines, could not stand on her own, required a wheelchair and was totally dependent for almost everything. She could not move her left arm, hand or fingers. Last night we went to Christmas Eve Service, she can walk, run, drive, is off all prescription drugs with the exception of a recent one which we hope is a temporary fix to help with a fluttering eye issue that has cropped up.

At this point she has regained limited movement in her left arm, occasional movement in her left hand and fingers. She continues to work so very hard and is determined to overcome her physical limitations. Your continued prayers for her total and complete recovery are greatly appreciated.

Her attitude is beyond remarkable. She exudes her faith and appreciation in everything she does and everyone she touches. Though she has suffered greatly over this last year, she is thankful for the many blessings that these circumstances have brought her. Knowing she has a family, fiancée and many friends that continue to support and pray for her. She has completed all but one class to earn her bachelor degree this spring, being featured in a TV commercial for UPMC (airing late January early February), recognized as "Out-patient of the year at Harmarville Rehabilitation and is going to be part of a series on encouragement at our church.

Today we celebrate GOD's gift of Christ's birth and the beginning of his life on earth. He has also given us the gifts of Heather's life, stronger faith, renewed hope and shown us true love.

May God bless you and your families.

Merry Christmas,

Randy Abramovic.

Heather Update – February 1, 2014

Friends,

For those of you in the UPMC viewing area.

Wanted to let everyone know that while Heather's commercial is not done yet a quick part will actually air during the Super Bowl. There is an ad for UPMC that starts," On a day where we recognize champions..."She is the second person, but watch quick as she is only on for about 2 seconds. Will miss you all tonight. Did want to share a praise, Heather has applied to UPMC for an internship this summer. She had a phone interview this week and it so happened that the person interviewing her is a Northway member and saw her testimony last weekend. Saw God's hand in that one!

Heather was featured at our church as part of the teaching sermon. So, I have attached the (2) short clips of her for your viewing.

https://vimeo.com/84910633

https://vimeo.com/84910984

For the entire message which I believe is wonderfully done here is the link.

http://www.youtube.com/watch?v=YZ0t8gU00s8&feature=youtu.be

I cannot express how appreciative and blessed we are for Heather to have made such improvements over the 14 months. Yet she still has a long way to go. We appreciate your continued prayers and support.

Randy Abramovic.

Heather Update – March 4, 2014

Friends,

Would like to share a wonderful moment with you. The attached video shows Heather's continued ability to have some return of movement in her left hand during a therapy session with Lynn. This gives us all great encouragement and hope for continued recovery.

She continues to work with the (Bioness) twice daily. The technology is amazing and a blessing. To watch her open her fingers and move her wrist with the assistance is a miracle. Unfortunately for us, we were told before Christmas that the insurance company had approved its purchase. About six weeks ago, they are now claiming it is "experimental" and is not covered. We are committed to helping Heather no matter what that takes. Please pray for the insurance company to realize the need and the benefit.

Heather has been experiencing some double vision and fluttering of her left eye. We saw a neurologist and he believe the eye tremors are temporary and actually caused by her brain healing. We are so thankful for that diagnosis also. She is able to control it with a prism on her glasses and a medication.

It is 15 months today since her brain surgery. We continue to be amazed by Heather's faith and determination to overcome her disabilities. She is in her last semester of college and is looking forward to graduating and getting out in the world. She is having her second interview for a paid internship with UPMC on Monday, March 10th please pray for her success. We are being told that her commercial will be released anytime now with UPMC. You may have caught a glimpse of it on the Super Bowl Sunday right after the half time show. It was an abbreviated spot along with 4 others as a campaign launch. She looks amazing.

We know how very blessed we all are, GOD has a wonderful plan for Heather and our family. It is so evident in having her here with us and seeing her progress. She is a true testament to strength, courage and a love for Jesus Christ.

Thank you all for your continued prayers and support. It is so greatly appreciated and helping.

My sincere thanks to all of you.

Randy Abramovic.

Heather Update – April 12, 2014

Friends,

It is a beautiful day in Pittsburgh and Lynn and I have just returned from a walk with Heather. **FIVE Miles,** around North Park Lake in 1 hour and fifteen minutes. As I walked behind her, I could not be more thankful and feel blessed. It was just 16 months since her brain surgery and 14 months since we brought her home in a wheelchair and totally dependent.

She was selected for the final round of interviews (15 people), from 900 applicants, for an internship with UPMC. Unfortunately, did not get one of the 9 openings. But was told to apply after graduation for possible Human Resource Management positions. Disappointed, but understanding that she did her best and that there will be other opportunities.

The next day she heard from IUP that she still needs two more classes to graduate. We are now scrambling to help her find housing to take one class in May for three weeks. Then take her last undergraduate class on line to finish up between now and August. She is so determined and focused to do well and finish her education strong and well as she has done all along.

Heather's TV commercial was launched this week and I have attached a link to it for your viewing. I think it turned out beautifully and captures her spirit.

http://www.youtube.com/watch?v=a90wS_-6oLs&list=UUieW-cGaXf-a2z0ADF-OoCqQ

Please continue prayers for Heather, her continued recovery, direction in life, as she finishes school, gets married in October and explores opportunities on how she may use her traumatic experiences to help others.

As always, I cannot thank you all enough, for your continued prayers and support. It has been a very challenging time. Yet GOD has given us peace when we most needed it, laughs when we wanted to cry and always felt his love.

Randy Abramovic.

Heather Update – May 10, 2014

Friends,

Yesterday I had the opportunity to go to Heather's therapy and wanted to share a photo to show that she continues to improve in strength and function. It is such a miracle to watch her work so hard mentally and physically to do tasks we often take for granted. Yet her bold determination continues to inspire us all. I have attached a photo of Heather lifting and moving a one pound can yesterday with assisted stimulation. We are truly encouraged by her limited function.

Heather and her mom have now decided to train together with an app "From Couch To 5 K" and are running / walking together. Which brings me to another reason for this note today on the eve of Mother's Day. As proud of Heather as I am. Lynn has been there every moment. From the weeks of staying by her side in the hospital to today (17 Months since brain surgery). She is such a great mother. Selfless in all she does and always ready to do whatever it takes to support her family. We often talk about how none of us could have gotten through this very difficult time without our faith in Jesus Christ. Knowing how blessed we are to have Lynn as mom and wife.

Please continue to pray for Heather's continued recovery. For her successful completion of her last two college classes this summer and for direction on where God wants her to share and use her difficult life experiences to help others in the future.

To all our friends that are mothers, I wish you the best. If possible, please give each of your children an extra hug and let them know how very special they are to you and what a blessing child are no matter what the circumstances may be.

As always, thank you very much for your continued prayers and support.

Randy Abramovic.

Heather Update – October 12, 2014

Friends,

I realize that it has been months since my last Heater Update and for that I apologize.

Yesterday Heather and Greg. were married, it was perfect in all respects. The following is my Father of the bride speech. I believe this captures the essence of where Heather has been and where she is going.

Father of the Bride Wedding Speech

Randy Abramovic; Daughter Heather

10/11/14

Ladies and gentlemen, friends, and family – good evening!!! If there is anyone here that doesn't know me, my name is Randy Abramovic **(ASK, Lynn to Stand**) and this is...Lynn my beautiful wife of 35 years--- we are Heather's proud parents.

It is a huge honor and privilege to be standing here today, welcoming you to the wedding of Heather and Greg. I especially thank those of you that have traveled from out of town to help us celebrate. Along with a very special thank you to Dr. Friedlander, who was Heather's neurosurgeon.

With all sincerity – thank you all!!

As I am sure you all know, we almost lost Heather about 22 months ago and there is not a day that goes by that I do not thank GOD for saving her. In ICU GOD shared a very clear vision of her with me. **First,** she was walking down the isle of her sister Lauren's wedding... she did it, **second,** we were walking down the isle of her wedding, we did today. The **third** vision, well let's say you need to check back in 9 months or more for that one. You'll be calling me "GRANDY" ⋯. Through this vision GOD told me... "Tell Heather to go and have a wonderful life" ⋯. Today is another huge step in that direction for Heather and Greg's wonderful life together.

I have been instructed by Heather several times "DAD, NO CRYING" and Keep the speech Short and sweet" ⋯ so I promise I'll do my best.

Heather and Greg have certainly experienced many up and downs in their young lives. Yet they both have shown **incredible Strength, Faith and Love through it all.**

To think it all began at Greg's fraternity house at IUP in April of 2010. Heather and a friend had just got to the party and his first words to Heather "we're out of beer." He is such a sweet talker. With a grand gesture Heather responded with, that is OK, I have a box of wine in my purse. Even though Heather made such a great impression on Greg he had forgotten her name and could only remember that it started with an 'H'. He did capture her phone number and eventually figured out the name.

On October 6th, 2012 a very nervous Greg. proposed while catching a bowl of soup in his lap.

If he hadn't noticed, Heather has an **amazing independent spirit**. Since she was a little girl she would say "I DO IT". Then in many cases she would. She is so dedicated and determined. She began riding horses when she was 2 and half years old. She competed in hunter Jumper show rings for about 20years. Recently she decided if I can't compete in hunter jumpers due to my limited function my left arm and hand, I'll do barrel racing because you hold the reins in your right hand. So much for that plan she fell and broke her left arm just a couple of months ago.

Heather is **so very smart.** When she was in second grade, we would get the girls a gift or treat of some kind to celebrate their accomplishments in school. Heather asked for me to take a horseback riding lesson. She knew if she could hook me into liking horses her chances of getting a horse someday were greatly increased. We did. When Heather was 10 and we were visiting her GOD Father, Vince Lyons in Atlanta and enjoying their boat at the time. Vince and I were talking about Las Vegas and Heather overheard the discussion and asked if I would take her there for her 21st birthday. I agreed and she proceeded to write it down on a napkin and have me sign it. To make a long story short, about 10 years later she pulled that napkin out. We wound up with eight of us in Las Vegas celebrating Heather 's 21st.

This December Heather will officially graduate from IUP with academic honors with a Cumulative GPA of 3.7 even after all of her setbacks in her senior year.

TURN TO HEATHER & Greg

What a **beautiful woman you have become**. Both inside and out. Greg you are one lucky guy. Both of you have shown faith and love through many trails as a true-life partnership already.

As Heather's father, I have prayed every day of her life for a man to come into her life that would love, honor and provide for her. My prayers have been answered by Greg. Lynn and I are proud to call Heather our daughter, we are proud to call him our son-in law.

RAISE A GLASS & TOAST

It gives me great pleasure to toast this marriage, wishing the two of you a wonderful life together. If all the guests would please join me in offering a toast to the newly married couple.

PAUSE

HEATHER & GREG

May you be blessed with a STRONG FAITH, UNENDING HOPE and TRUE LOVE forever!

Please continue to pray for Heather and Greg as they move into this next phase of their life journey as a married couple.

Randy Abramovic.

Heather Update – December 2, 2014

Friends,

Today marks the second-year anniversary of Heather's lifesaving brain surgery. Such a blessing to have her with us and doing so well. A couple of highlights are she finished undergraduate work at IUP with honors. She got married on October 11 to a fine young man who has been with her for the last four years and never wavered. Three weeks ago, she joined our marketing firm as an HR and Marketing Assistant.
Heather wrote this today and I thought it captures the situation perfectly.

"Whelp, it's that day. Two years ago, today, I underwent a lifesaving

9-hour brain surgery to save my life and remove a cavernous Angioma from my brain stem. I woke from surgery unable to move the entire left side of my body but I was alive! I can't believe all this happened to me, but I have faith that God will use this for good and for His glory. I am so grateful for how far I've come and all those people who helped me get through the hardest time in my life. This disease, cavernous angioma, has no cure and no treatment. We need to change this. Yes, I still have deficits from all this, but I am so blessed. It could be so much worse. My husband and family love me, support me, and push me as I continue through my journey of recovery. This day will always be the mark of my old life ending, but a more grateful, beautiful, blessed life beginning!"

Heather Update – March 11, 2015

Friends,

Praise the LORD!!! Heather had her annual MRI today. We could not be happier and feel more blessed than to hear all is clear and Dr Friedlander feels she is doing wonderfully. What she has accomplished over the past 27 months through her faith in GOD, hard work and determined spirit are nothing short of a miracle.

Heather has entered a video competition in the 2015 Neuro Film Festival, which is sponsored by the American Academy of Neurology. The objective is to draw public awareness about the brain and nervous system diseases and the need for research in the United States and Canada. She should hear about how she did over the next few weeks. The conference and festival are in Washington DC in April.

This link is the video submitted to the Film Festival;

Video live at: http://youtu.be/yjSkNGSN3Lw

Please pray for Heather to continue to improve physically. For GOD to give her a clear understanding and path on how he would like her to use his blessings to help others.

Thank you all for your continued prayers and support. It is so greatly appreciated and helping.

My sincere thanks to all of you.

Randy Abramovic.

Heather Update – May 11, 2015

Friends,

Today Heather had an operation on her left Achilles tendon to lengthen it. The goal is to even out her gate and help her to walk more smoothly. The doctor feels that things went very well and feels her prognosis is very good.

She is being held at Mercy Hospital overnight to monitor her pain. At this point she is in very good spirits and tells me, "it's not brain surgery". She will be in a leg cast for six weeks and then a walking boot for six weeks.

Please pray for Heather's fast recovery and ultimate abilities recovery. For GOD to continue to bless her while she continues to strive to be the best she can be and help others along her life's journey.

Thank you all for your continued prayers and support. It is so greatly appreciated and helping.

My sincere thanks to all of you.

Randy Abramovic.

Heather Update – January 11, 2017

Friends,

I realize it has been too long since I have written and sent an update on Heather and I apologize.

Today Heather went through her follow up MRI as planned (Fourth

Year Since Brain Surgery). The area where she had the Cavernous Malformation is stable which means there is no sign of it and all is good. After her surgery, she got MRI'S after 4 months, 6 months and then one-year intervals. Today, Dr Friedlander her surgeon, lifesaver and a friend told her to stop in and see him anytime, but he didn't go to schedule another MRI for two years. Thank you, Jesus.

I am so very proud of her, her faith in GOD, her strength and courage to not let this hinder her in her life endeavors. As in all of life's challenges Heather is showing all of us how to take every day as the blessing it is and to make the most of every day. To not be concerned about the little inconveniences we encounter, but to step up and make a difference in this thing we all call life. I cannot be more proud of my daughter and I too have committed to her to use her experience as my catalyst to live my life to the fullest. To truly look to Jesus Christ for my guidance and act in accordance.

Over these four years she has completed her undergraduate work with honors, gotten married and is working in her field of HR Management. She and Greg just sold their home in Regent Square in one day for full asking price and bought a new home in Hampton of which they will be moving into at the end of this month. The buyer did not want an inspection and it is a cash deal. If there were ever a young couple that God was showing his glory it is Greg and Heather and they are certainly deserving.

While she and Greg were talking with Dr. Friedlander and getting caught up on life in general Heather mentioned that they have been "talking about starting a family". The great doctor's response to them was "you need to do more than talk". I thought I was going to wet my pants laughing. But he is a doctor and should know.

Workbook

In this section of the book, you can use the questions to reflect on your own journey.

Chapter One: The Dawn; Heather talks about her life growing up and things that helped shape her into the adult she became. Use the questions below to identify your foundation and goals in life you have:

1. *Make a list of life events or experiences you had growing up that you feel impacted you in some way, could be positive or negative. Under each event, write down in a couple sentences in what way these events impacted you.*

   _____
   _____
   _____
   _____
   _____

2. *Make a list of all the things you have in your life (be simplistic here, i.e. roof over my head, food, clothes, etc.) Then make a list of the wants you have, but I want you to title this list Goals. and under each goal, write a brief sentence of how you can attain this goal. This will shift our focus on taking control of our wants instead of focusing on the fact we don't have them*

   _____
   _____
   _____
   _____
   _____

Chapter Two: The Love; Heather talks about meaningful relation-ships she had in her life. She believes these relationships had signifi-cance in continuing to shape her life. Use these questions to reflect on meaningful relationships you've had in your life.

1. *Write down in a couple sentences your first real relationship, the "love" one*

    _____
    _____
    _____
    _____
    _____

2. *What were some red flags of this relationship you chose to ignore but wish you hadn't then?*

    _____
    _____
    _____
    _____
    _____

3. *Write down a couple names of men/women whom you dated or were friends with, who were impactful in your life (could be good or bad), and then next to their name, write down what you learned from that relationship.*

    _____
    _____
    _____
    _____
    _____

Chapter Three: The Big Debut; Heather finds out about the "demon" living inside her head. Use the questions below to reflect on the life-changing news that you've received in your life:

1. *Make a list of your "world stopper" moments in your life and a sentence or two describing them*

_____
_____
_____
_____
_____

2. *Under each "world stopper", write down the characteristic about yourself that you learned from it happening to you*

_____
_____
_____
_____
_____

3. *More likely than not, this "world stopper" took your life on a different path than you would have imagined. Write down a couple sentences of how it changed your life*_____

_____
_____
_____
_____

4. *Write down a couple sentences of how you think your life would be different if this "world stopper" did not happen (include the bad and the good here)*

_____
_____

_____

_____

_____

Chapter Four: The Puzzle; Heather is faced with a very big decision. Her decision could immensely affect the rest of her life. Use these questions to identify life changing decisions you have faced

1. *In times of stress, what are some activities or outlets you use to escape your reality?*

    _____

    _____

    _____

    _____

    _____

2. *What has been the biggest puzzle of your life? What was the outcome?*

    _____

    _____

    _____

    _____

Chapter Five: The Chaos; Heather compares the plan she had for her life to the reality of what was happening to her. She also starts to question her decision not to have the brain surgery and what would have been if she did. Use these questions to examine your life plan compared to your reality.

1. *What was your plan for your life? What is your realty?*

_____
_____
_____
_____
_____

2. Describe a time you had to make a tough decision and then later questioned the decision you made?

_____
_____
_____
_____
_____

3. Have you ever been dealing with something that an outside stranger couldn't tell by looking at you? Did people treat you differently?

_____
_____
_____
_____
_____

Chapter Six: The Nightmare; Heather is now faced with struggling through her bleak diagnosis and the unknown of what may lie ahead. Also, she soon had one of her worst nightmares happen out of her control. Use these questions to identify ways you have coped with life situations and your perspective to them.

1. What is/was a situation you changed your perspective to help cope?

   _____

   _____

   _____

   _____

2. Talk about a life event that happened to you that you are glad you didn't know was going to happen beforehand?

   _____

   _____

   _____

   _____

   _____

3. What was your reaction to that event and was it how you'd expect to react?

   _____

   _____

   _____

   _____

   _____

4. If your reaction was different than expected, explain why you think this happened.

   _____

   _____

   _____

   _____

   _____

Chapter Seven: The Grit; Heather woke up from brain surgery in a new body that was much different than the one she knew before the stroke. She was at the beginning of the biggest battle of her life. Use these questions to point out your own strengths when facing times of great difficulty.

1. *Name a time you reacted to a situation/circumstance and wish you could have reacted differently. What was your reaction and how would you do it differently?*

     _____

     _____

     _____

     _____

     _____

2. *Name a time you encountered difficulty in your life and took it head on with determination.*

     _____

     _____

     _____

     _____

     _____

3. *What motivates you through difficult times in your life?*

     _____

     _____

     _____

     _____

     _____

4. *Name a time you hit rock bottom in your life and what got you out of that?*

     _____

     _____

     _____

     _____

     _____

5. *Do you allow yourself to rest when your body calls for it?*

_____

_____

_____

_____

_____

Chapter Eight: The New Normal; Heather spends lots of time in the inpatient rehab facility but the day finally comes where she gets to go home and experience her new life outside the walls of the hospital. Use these questions to lay out goals you've had and the steps you took to accomplish them.

1. *Describe a time when you had negative thoughts that were irrational? What was the situation, what did you think, and what was the actual reality?*

_____

_____

_____

_____

2. *Name a big goal you have in life.*

_____

_____

_____

_____

_____

3. *What are smaller goals you can set on the way to achieve the big goal?*

_____

_____

_____

_____
_____

Chapter Nine: The Champion; Heather inspires and encourages people with her fight through outpatient physical therapy. She starts to finally accept her new reality of being disabled. Use these questions to discover ways you have adapted to your own realty.

1. *Describe a time someone gave you news that you weren't expecting, how did you handle it?*
   _____
   _____
   _____
   _____
   _____

2. *How have you adapted to giving up the way you pictured your life would be?*

   _____
   _____
   _____
   _____
   _____

Chapter Ten: The Great Leap; Heather is faced with a few setbacks and surgeries to help improve her life and recovery. The wedding day comes and is perfect. Use these questions to examine some setbacks you have encountered on your journey.

1. *When has life pulled you backwards?*
   _____
   _____

_____
_____

2. *What did the backwards motion propel you forward to?*

_____
_____
_____
_____
_____

Chapter Eleven: The New Beginning; Heather is starting her life after graduating from college and beginning her career and marriage, while having to undergo many more surgeries to help improve her quality of life. Use these questions to discuss ant recurrent bad times you've had or irrational fears you've faced.

1. *Tell me about a time you have felt like "bad things" kept happening to you and you couldn't catch a break*

_____
_____
_____
_____
_____

2. *If those bad things are over, what have you learned from them?*

_____
_____
_____
_____
_____

3. *Name a time you had irrational fear or anxiety over something that ended up not being as bad as you thought it was going to be?*

_____
_____
_____
_____
_____

Chapter Twelve: The Phoenix; Heather talks about her future and things that are currently going on in her life. She is able to look back on what she has been through and reflect on the detour her life took. Use these questions to reflect on your own life's detours and what you have gained from this book.

1. *What detours has life thrown you?*

_____
_____
_____
_____
_____

2. *What did you learn to appreciate more in life due to those detours?*

_____
_____
_____
_____
_____

3. *What was your biggest takeaway from this book?*

_____
_____
_____
_____
_____

4.   *What do you wish the author would've expanded on?*

_____

_____

_____

_____

_____

5.   *How can you apply this book to your life?*

_____

_____

_____

_____

_____

ABOUT
KHARIS PUBLISHING

KHARIS PUBLISHING is an independent, traditional publishing house with a core mission to publish impactful books, and channel proceeds into establishing mini-libraries or resource centers for orphanages in developing countries, so these kids will learn to read, dream, and grow. Every time you purchase a book from Kharis Publishing or partner as an author, you are helping give these kids an amazing opportunity to read, dream, and grow. Kharis Publishing is an imprint of Kharis Media LLC. Learn more at https://www.kharispublishing.com.

CPSIA information can be obtained
at www.ICGtesting.com
Printed in the USA
BVHW090242221220
596050BV00008B/19